ODES *& fragments*

ellipsis

• • •

press

ODES & fragments © 2013 Alan Davies

Thanks to those who first published these poems –
in chapbooks –
ODES / Faux Press / Jack Kimball
a token is a thinkg upon a tongue / Sona Books / Jill Magi
Always Within / Other Publications / Alan Davies
and magazines –
All Small Caps / Jess Mynes – Boog City / Laura Elrick & David Kirschenbaum & Christina Strong – The Broadkill Review / Jamie Brown – The Brooklyn Rail / Anselm Berrigan – Cannot Exist / Andy Gricevich – Exchange Values, The Final XIV Interviews + 1 / Tom Beckett – Mad Hatters' Review / Carol Novack – mark(s) / Ted Pearson & Deb King – Ocho / Nick Piombino & Didi Menendez – Onedit / Tim Atkins – Otoliths / Mark Young – Process / David Rich & Lisa Reynolds Rich – The Recorder / Jess Mynes & Stephen Broll – Vanitas / Vincent Katz – West Wind Review / Sarah Cunningham

Author photo / Kenji Kiritani

First Edition
ISBN 0-9637536-8-1
ISBN-13 978-0-9637536-8-7

Distributed to the trade by Small Press Distribution, Berkeley, California
Toll-free number (US only): 800-869-7553
Bay area / International: 510-524-1668
orders@spdbooks.org
www.spdbooks.org

Ellipsis Press, LLC
PO Box 721196
Jackson Heights, NY 11372
www.ellipsispress.com

OTHER BOOKS by ALAN DAVIES

slough cup hope tantrum

SPLIT THIGHS

a an av es

ABUTTAL

MNEMONOTECHNICS

ACTIVE 24 HOURS

PURSUE VERITABLE SIMPLES/SEND US THE DIFFICULT JOBS

NAME

SIGNAGE

CANDOR

LIFE

an untitled collaboration with M M Winterford

RAVE

PANTHER

Sei Shonagon

SERENITY

PAIN

Don't Know Alan (with Miles Champion)

Book 2

Book 3 / BAD DAD

LESLIE SCALAPINO ÷ ALAN DAVIES

BOOK 5

BOOK 6

ODES

a token is a thinkg upon a tongue

NOM

Always Within

Raw War

ODES *& fragments*

ALAN DAVIES

CONTENT

AND NEITHER IS THERE PAIN — 13
FOR GOING AWAY IS TO STAY — 23
SLOOPING DOWN THE LONG SLOPE TOWARD — 30
AS IF WERE NOT OTHERWISE OR SO — 35
TODAY AS A WAY OF ESCLAPE — 38
AS ERR AS FAR AS FAR CAN SEE — 43
STEAMING INTO PLANGENT HARBOR — 44
IT ALL FALLS AWAY — 63
AND IT WAS — 65
A BODY LOVES A BODY IN ITS NAME — 67
FOR VALENTINE ACKLAND — 70
THERE ARE DAYS WITH FLOCKS OF ROSES — 71
GLASSINE IS A COLOR TO THE WANDERING EYE — 72
WITH NOTHING NEW TO SAY — 73
DIODE — 75
WE'RE MOVING FORWARD DOWN THE THEN — 93
THRALLDOM — 95
FOR FERNANDA — 96
THRAKE RALLDOM RIDDLE AND CRASH — 104
FOR YOU'N — 106
MY THINGER ARE FLINGLETS — 107
THINKEN — 108
AND IS ALL A THRALL A BELL — 111
OH SINK UPON A TONGUE OF FIRE — 112
IT ENDS — 113
VELVET — 114
I THINK IT IS SAFE TO SAY — 117
THERE WE SEQUESTER OURSELVES — 126
TAKE THRALL — 134
IT'S A SLOW MOAN — 135
I'M REMEMBERING YOU AS OVERLETS — 139
THINKGS — 142
WE SOMETIMES STUMBLE FOOL — 145
FAMILY DAY — 146
SHINES — 148
A TOKEN IS A THINKG UPON A TONGUE — 150
A PALLIATIVE IS A THING — 168
IT'S 7:44 — 169
BEING MOMENTLESS UPON A SEA — 176
FEMINA — 178
AND THEN WE TURN — 179
REMEMBERING THE THRELL — 180
SWARMSY — 182
SIGNED — 184
SLACKENED AND THEN BITTEN — 185

That's laying back — 186
it's all over now — 188
once in a blue moon — 189
Harp Object — 192
nothing is as worthless — 193
Dirndl — 203
To give phenomenology a name — 209
The moments that haven't got moments in them — 212
and the glassed in days — 215
Stone — 219
where there is bottomlessness — 231
Past the asking — 232

<u>And neither is there pain</u>

For Christina

And neither is there pain

An horrible thing, again

The harsh thralldom

Secreting momentless agony

Over the sensate thrust

Magically momentless

And lost, lost over losings

Where trials seal logics

Against the willed moment

Orphaned and again, then

The silent sluice of trust

Not that there is / was trust

Thrust, the gainless moment

Sacrificed by dams, thrown

And the agentless moment

Sequestered against semen

And the lost marbled age

Truncated that abets ages

Against ages, and all against

The thrust of mommy and

Aghast oh it was dead that

One, the thrall, the thicket

Taken over trumpeting

Tickets taxed beyond recall

Or over the over the over

And that, suddenly suggest

Or eager or buttressed or

Ore, or against the sad twixt

Momentless dead thangers

Not that things mattered

In mixed companionless

Ways halved hexed and

Hardened over eagerless

Leagues, let nothing happen

As happens, or equals un

Equal to all that happens,

Appears and sweaters the

Mixed up sadness concrete

And concreted against foul

Thickened squirts, or the

Over party gets guts it's not

Had to have that way, not

Over that way, ever, and

The dead dead dear guts

Of staunch dead dear guts

Or the sealed over parties

Of that being there and

That being that, there, and

There, being, that, there

Or there were orgies over the

Olives and the olive branches

Branched over the orgies

And all coming was come

And all come was coming over

The orgies, the olive branches

In the Roman sense of that

Or Greek, doesn't matter, just

That things were once things

And're now things, maybe

Again, or maybe not things,

Again, like leaseless dead

Matters hardening over

Harvests at any time of year

That bakes makes things

Into what can be used to

Be what is of no use, what

Will never be of any use, not

Now, not ever, there's that

That has to be considered

Inconsiderately over the

Had match beaconing slick

Where slick might happen

Might never happen, might

And the egregious matter

At hand is hand, is hand

And the hand is not the

Egregious matter but is

Is the hand, the hand, only

Shall we say that, need we

Say that, only the hand, no

The hand, enough stood

Against the arbor fettered

From cowboys and cowgirls

Beating their selves cowish

In the cowed light, against

All other lights, no light, and

Light, walking eagerly over

The sands, almost said stands

What matter the walking, the

Over, the walking over, the

Toward, the ward, the to, the

Toward you, you, you, the one

Over, over toward, to, to

And all that slushes up

Is not slush, but eagerness

Or the half-life of larvae, or

The larvae living more than

Half a life, given the off-chance

That larvae exist, that life

Happens, happens to larvae

I don't know, there's the trip

Up the side of the trip up

And the casual abandonment

Of abandoning what is casual

For what is abandoned, in

Other words, the way things

Are, the way things usually

Are, and against that, if there

Is a that, if that is a that, the

Momentless, momentless

Again, again, surety of happen

Stances, held up against the

Walls, walls of help, held up

Against help as if that were not

A place that it might be

Agreeable to be, for someone

If there were a someone, a

Someone who might be

Agreeable to be, shaking

Shaking the specterless

Shilled moments of shaken

Abutments that slack, sick

Over the warded harvesters

Maxing out at masked balls

With millions of nothings

As the target, the reward, and

The happenstance, the simple

Happenstance, of being there

Or there were old organdies

Presuming organs in the slick

Stilt mire of growing things

Emaled and over all that the

Formed female femaled where

Washing occurs without stop

Or surcease, stop, or, surcease

Letting legendary morphs get

Imageless in the larded stiff

Stuff of stiff stuff, stuff stiff

With the energyless morphing

Of energy, morphing, swept

Scepterless across the scanned

Dunes where hard hearts hit

Morphed runes and accept

Imageless torqued splendors

Sitting unequal to nothing on

The lady like ends of all that

Ends, of what ends, and the

Grim sequences of stilton

Eaten, eating itself really

Over the glens of fens and

Under the trip wire that sends

Warmth where warmth is

Needed most, between, where

Where, and we know it all, there

Is nothing we don't know, nothing

We do know, all, there is only all,

Fomenting change, and change

Less ness, the sad ventriloquistic

Morphing of getting, a sad

A sad thing happening only

Under ground, where ground

Grows, but knows, but knows

Nothing, *This Is The End*

FOR GOING AWAY IS TO STAY

FOR GOING AWAY IS TO STAY

AS IF THERE WERE ANOTHER DAY

IN THIS HALCYON THIS MOST HALCYON

OF AWKWARD SPACES, CACKLING

AS SKWAWKING DOES IN THE THRALL

OF EASTERLY MORONIC SEPTEMBERISH

SPACES THAT GRAFT THE SEADRIFT

FROM THE LAND INTO SKY, THE FAST

DEATH WISH THAT DEATH WISHES FOR

AGAINST ALL THAT HASN'T AND ALL THAT HAS

BEEN SAID OVER THE SAD ABYSMAL

AUGUSTINE SLEEPOVER ISLANDS, WHERE

CASKS OF MEMORY LOSE THEMSELVES

IN THE SNOT OF HISTORY, AS IF HOSPITALITY

COULD EVOKE PENITENCE OR TURN BACK

WHAT IS ALREADY BACK, WHAT IS ALREADY

TURNED, AND WHAT CAN'T BE HAD, NOT

IN A MILLION TEARS, MY DEAR, NOT AS

YOU SWEAT YOUR HANDS FOR THIRST

IN THE EAGLETTING HORROR THAT SMACKS

OF SMACK, OR THE THRIFT GALLED SMUT

GLUTTING HARVESTS WHERE FOOD IS

NEEDED FOR THE FOODLESS, MEDICINE

FOR THE MEDICINELESS, PEACE FOR THE

PEACELESS, AND SO ON, GET IT

AGAINST THE DEAD HEAD RECKONING

OF WHAT CAN'T BE RECKONED, WHAT

CAN'T BE HAD, TOLERATED SECONDED

OR VOTED OUT OF OFFICE, THE ORIFICE

IS TOO SMALL A TARGET FOR EVEN

THE MOST BLASTEDLY BLISSFUL OF

BULLETS, HURRY, THEN GHASTLY THINGS

START UP IN THE FURNACE, THE HEAT

RISES AND SETTLES TO ICE ALL ALONG

THE DANUBIAL LACKLUSTER SPECTRES

OF GRIPPING HAPPENSTANCE AND

GREED AS THE SWEATERED FEW

GREET THEMSELVES OVER HAND

SHAKES AND HANKIES AND THE ODD

GLASS OF WHAT OTHERS CAN'T AFFORD

TO DRINK, THE TROUGH BEING EMPTY

FOR ALL BUT THE TROOPS AND THEIR

HERALDED (THEIR SELF HERALDED)

MASTERS GATHERING ALONG THE BANKS

OF ALL OF EACH AND EVERY RIVER

AS THEY ADVANCE TOWARD THEMSELVES

ON HORSEBACK, THE UNCHOSEN FEW

SPITTING ONE LAST TIME BEFORE THEY

BOARD THE SHIPS FOR OTHER PLACES

PLACES THAT DON'T EXIST, GUTTER DEAD

SLOP FUCKED ASS CRAP MASTERS

LOOMING OUT OF THE SCHOOLS THEY

WENT TO AND CREAKING TOWARD THE

CASKETS THEY ATTEND (NOT THEIR OWN)

AS IF AN ANGELIC CHOIR COULD SAVE US

(PAST TENSE) BUT IT CAN'T, NOT AGAINST

THE CLAWED SPECTRISH APING THAT

EVEN ART NOW DOES ON THE WALLS

OF THE PENITENT CATHEDRALS OF SPACE

(ART), WHERE BUFFETING ONCE, ONLY

A FEW WEEKS AGO, SOMETHING LIKE

HOPE HOPED THERE WAS SOMETHING

LIKE HOPE, ALAS, ALAS, ALAS, AND THE

WEEKENDING FEW EAT THEIR PEANUTS

BESIDE THE RHINE OR CHESEPEAKE BAY

AND HAVE NOTHING ELSE TO SAY, NO

NOTHING ELSE TO SAY, NOT REALLY,

EXCEPT THAT AS THE LAST OF US WAVES

GOODBYEGOODBYE TO THE LAST OF US

WE KNOW ONLY ONE THING WHAT WAS IT

OH YEAH THAT WAS IT WHAT WAS IT WAS IT

WORTH REMEMBERING WHAT WAS IT WAS

THERE ONE THING DID WE EVER KNOW IT

DID WE EVER REMEMBER IT I'M DEDICATING

THIS TO YOU NANCY AS AGAINST ALL

THAT HAS HAPPENED SINCE, HAS ANYTHING

HAPPENED SINCE, I DON'T THINK SO, WHAT I

WHAT SO, WHAT THINK, THE ALL OF IT GOING

DOWN THE SLIDE INTO THE SLIDE, INTO

THE DOWN INTO, INTO THE DOWN, INTO THE

INTO, PURLOINED, PARBOILED, ROTTEN,

ROTTEN IN THE FLESH DRY ROT SETTING IN

INTO THE HARVEST OF A COUNTRY AT A LOSS

A COUNTRY AT A LOSS FOR PEOPLE, THE PEOPLE

STARVING FOR PEOPLE, NOW THAT'S A WAY

TO HAVE THAT, TO HAVE THAT BEING THAT

A WAY TO HAVE THAT BE ALL OVER THAT

WITHOUT THERE BEING A CHANCE OF A THING

HAPPENING, NOTHING, ZILCH, NOT A THING

GOING ON GOING AWAY GOING A WAY

TO GET IT GOING, SLENDER CHANCE

SLENDER PICKENS IN THE HERBARIAL

GARDEN, NOTHING TO EAT THIS YEAR ALL

GONE IN THE BUCKETS OF THE OTHERS

AS THE 800 HERE AND THE 8,000 THERE

AND THE 800,000 THERE JUST GO AWAY

JUST GO AWAY, JUST GO AWAY INTO

THE GUTLESS FEW, UNSPICED, EATEN WHOLE

GONE, GONE THE WAY OF A WHOLE PERSON

THE WHOLE WAY OF A WHOLE POPULATION

A WHOLE GENERATION, A WHOLE SEVERAL

GENERATIONS IN SOME CASES, GONE GONE

DARFUR RWANDA GUANTAMO BAY

THE BAY OF FUCKING PIGS FULL OF FUCKING

PIGS THIS TIME OF YEAR, THIS TIME NEXT

YEAR, ASSHOLES STUFFING THEIR ASSHOLES

FULL OF THE NOT-YET-DEAD, IE THE LIVING

GET IT THE LIVING EATING THE LIVING

EATING THE LIVING OFF THE LAND OF THE

NOT-YET-DEAD, SO MUCH NOT WORTH

BOTHERING ABOUT, OR SO MUCH JUST

IN THE WAY (INJUSTICE) JUST IN THE WAY

OF STUFF "WE" ("WE" "WE" "WE" "WE"

"WE") WANTWANTWANTWANTWANTWANT,

THERE'S NO TOMORROW FOR THAT KIND

OF GREED, FOR THAT KIND OF UNKIND GREED

THERE'S NO TOMORROW, NOT TODAY, NO,

NO TODAY EVEN, NOT FOR THAT KIND OF

GREED, THAT KIND OF CARELESS LACK OF

CARING, THAT KIND OF NOTHINGNESS

IN THE FACE OF NEED AND THE CARE WORN

BLIP FACES THAT LOSE THEMSELVES

OFF THE SCREEN BEFORE ANYBODY (ANY

OF THOSE WITH A SCREEN) GIVES A FLYING

FUCK INTO THE SICKENING CRYING AIR

FOR GOING AWAY IS TO STAY

30

Slooping Down the Long Slope Toward

Slooping down the long slope toward sloops

And finding uncanny reward in no reward

Nor in that either (neither), as we escape into

The timbrest of slad October airs, as a sweater

Becomes itself only when of no longer use

Or the bickering flux (flugs) matriculates us

Past what we weren't going to be anyway

Not out here, not past where we never got

And hadn't wanted to be, or to get anyway

We only know that the theater was invented

For tyrants and that we're in it and to have

Us in it, and that all kinds of slag fluds muck up

The hardship into calcitrant evecastors as a

Side way of doing what can't be done undone

Or even thought about again, not ever again

(No gain) so that the drag fwogs slup angle

Ions and the daily paperless harbinger swags

Fluck pastors down the dequestering swept

Streets (or are they steps) that we fall from

As angling after all of the thrilling slick stuff

We get out selves (our selves silly) stuck

In the unstuckness of the death that camps

Like a boot (lick that booty) in the maw cask

Slung drags, [This is for Antony & the Johnsons

May he one day grow up to be a beautiful girl]

And there are places they throw us and usus

And the getting there gets us all of a trump

So there's no hard on of the nardening past

Old garments given down by slump kind of

Jammy types cutletting up the sides of the beef

Consciousness of a state gone rampant and mad

Rampant and made, as an eager frag diligence

Gets lost over its own hardening sliced up

Into the ditches of dirges, where only the sillies

Get past the rest of us, clumpetting on and along

Into the slick curtains that pass for pastures

Or other places we can't have been not lately

There were days, could it be could enough to say

That, as against the harboring slankfasterers

Crumpetting up along the slides of what lives us

And into the taken tolds of what's token

The slottering wretches crumpetting over (again)

In pain, as over against the pained recalcitrance

That him em and clept them up the grunt sides

Of harbored grief, briefly as lived as a flint, as

Useless as a dod (wasn't) and then on into the

Furnace (yet to be lit) blited with flies and the

Glint stuff of grack smuck, oh it's turn over the

Time, it's turn over the time, slack up the crick

And fish the warren out of the warden's clock

Find a time, anytime find anytime, let that be

That, or (for grug's slake) something like that

Hastening into the furrows where we used to put

Our flicker fingers, when time was wet with its

Own whistle and our own part of it none of ours

To have to do with it, just the smarmering happen

Stance growling out of furtive ground toward up

Dance crackle thimble thing happening, no not,

Or up that toward the sheltering sky of sly re

Monstrance, the overt quickening of slink flu gag

Trig fraggerers, the old school type, the ones that

Went to school with themselves in the after

Math of the fore / math, the ones slought slang dug

And then did that, diditdiditdidit, up, up, up to us

How why what wherefore and all that, meaning

Less now in the slew of stew slaughtering its way

Around us (in search of us), and the slug doggerel

Flungking slangward (glangward) into the west

The best west we've got (left), really masterful

In its curtailment of itself of what it was is of what

Is it of what it might be of what it might become of

What it will be (will it be that) of what it will become

If becoming becomes it (it won't / it don't) as against

Them fluggerer frag slung drag olden klip slankerers

(Them ones / and don't you fucking forget it)

The ones with a vested interest in nothing but vested

Interest (them ones) as the sky strips itself bare

Of its elements in these latter days, latter than the

Last ones and, probably, even latterer than that

As the sky curves away from itself, and the earth

Too, and form shapes itself into formlessness

As against being nothing at all, and the pink pigeon

Pluck of what's up there (what might have been

Up there) gets caught in the lyrical moment

Of orgasming dearth (oh sad sad moment sad

Sad thing) and the flock glutterers shoot (shoo)

Them all out of the sky, in advance of they themselves

Wanting to be there, taking it all leaving nothing

Such that nothing is left nothing nothing at all

As If It Were Not Always Otherwise Or So

There is a platinum surcease of blonde cloud rising over the bond
Of Februarial months, even though this is not the ground
Of that or any other month, but the festooning pluralization
Of creaking things come to moan in the pleasant happenstances
Generating faith as if it had a furlough and could spend it anywhere
Regardless of faith or faithlessness, and the proud grand tours
Of old dames listening to Monteverdi after hours in after hour joints
On the other side of the river where no river is, but then there is
Contagion as a kind of recompense, an unkind kind of recompense
Really as against all that stuttering falls there, and galls the air
Of its ringlets of spruced time, pining after altars of quizzical small
Talk between vestry and vestment, there being no quaking in the hills
Of town tonight, with literal luckless hardscapes keeping us awake
From totemless tea things as if wishing could turn them, all that, to
Something worth taking from life, an afterthought maybe or the sling
Things that we give to one another when giving is not enough, when
Things are not enough, are not things, and the lucent slip sups of stuff
Are handed about like bandied ices over the mantles of curling
Spice, where more could not be said of more, nor less of less, even
If it were more, and where countless clues count for cluelessness

As aquarian old farts stutter up the ramps toward home, eagerly

In this flourish to be abetting there, as against the casks, the water

Baskets full of air, and bully for them, miraculous minestrone

Standing in for minuets and ministers of the radical forest type

As it stands on the page, meaning something as nothing means some

Thing, but that is not all, not in this graspless entered fall, it's May

And there is nothing more to say of what's faltering here, what's

Not even here, or can't be here, can't be gotten here, not even the

Grapes that push their own harvest into edible drinkable mouths

Conquering fashion as over against trails leaving tide marks on the

Eyes where eyes would be ears for the hearing, but no, the old young

Ones are getting up to be dead, starting to be staring past the lines

Of truncated and truncating blasphemes, crutchless, aching for a kind

Of morpheme that would not be invented yet but that would have

Meaning, that kind of morpheme, but not that kind of meaning maybe

As that would be a curtain over where other curtains fed the streams

Of gleaming meaning, the silvering threads of a line snorted into the

Dread slick clackers, the place where we can't go from, a kind of

Slick palimpsest set over the harbors of waters watering harbors

Boatless of sterns and boatless afts and the quick diurnal circadian

Lackluster widdershins going forward into backwardness, as we

As we cut short what was never long to begin with, the life of a flea

Lived on a round emblem, shaking, and diceless, and a cup in a hat

Floating downstream from the river to the sea, from the sea to the

River, and back up into the air, or the spigot, back into the blameless

Slack harbor, where mitigation slips unheard between the slim boards

Of lording crumpets, old school, and then back again to where there

Is no back and to where there is no again, neither gain nor back

But the slim slick crimp taken in time by one who dies, by one who

Only dies, there being no time before that for what might have been

Before that, had there been a before, had there been a that, but no

We're emblemless little tokens ourselves adrift, and that be that

As, swimming over the harvests of the little houses the big people

Take what's there, oh oh, and what isn't there, slippage as a swarm

Fest of treacle taken and tokened, the warm harvesters left behind

In the slim crack of the ancient rhymer, the slow casking baskets

Holding words, the element of time troughing into old man humps

So that, so that willingness is not willing, cannot be taken for that

Never was that, and never, never will be that, willing as one may be

In this elementless slime grasping the handles of the airs, oars

Or the slim sweet people empeopling the globe with happiness

Those moments that creak out of the hard past like lanterns lighting

The lake the large lake already largely lit by moon light, hurtling

Over the falls toward the vale, streaming with redolent personages

In redolent boats, or boaters, depending on the time of year, of life

As eagerly we slump into toward as if that's a destination as if that's

Destination enough for a crowd of crowding hungry cats, the little

People that make the words wing, sing, across the casketless wires

In flood or neap tide, wearing shirts down to their people holes

And the time changes as we think it does, and the hills have change

In them, and the river lets the banks slide past, and the ocean sloughs

In its cups and the sky skirts all else, and the trumpets of air inveigle

Sense out of the uneven ground, and the ground begs for mercy

On our behalf, and it's too late, it's too late, it's too late for all that

38

Today As A Way of Esclape

These vestal crested moments all but abet the time's moments

So cretinously full of spaced casing as against the aghast filigree

Specularly spacing itself over the tomb walkers spending days

Speeding against curtails and the emblems of slept walkers

Going away from away, toward form and the egoless basking

Of cakes into days, but for the gradual horizoning of plants over

Days as a kind of dusking supplants memory and the swept clean

Triumvirate separates all but itself from the terza rima of olde

Not that basking betters itself as an antiphon sleazing over the

Realmed slept squats of toned stuck stuff, that being the moment

As defined by the moment, in an abyss, and out of any abyss

At all oddly sneaking over toward the horizontal bars where drinks

Are quaffed vertically and the slay days itself into ineffable

Horizons (there are no horizons) as momentless slim offerings glib

Themselves up and demand something of the lingering populace

All but dead just from being the lingering populace and quite apart

From the sluck thingle quackers going over and aboard the bring

Boats that take nothing here (from there (or elsewhere)) there being

No here (not as the days slip themselves into absolution) and no there

(Not as the days slip themselves into dissolution) and no elsewhere (not

As the days slip just slip slip just slip the days just slip slip slip away)

A kind of casketless egolessness felt in all that, courageously wishing

There were wishes or that there were courage for that matter, or that

The courageous wishing had happened in the first place (hah!) for that

Matter, but butter only makes the bread look better it's all a beatific thing

That only tries to look us (us (to look us (too (to look us too)))) in the eyes

To lingeringly admit that nothing gets any better and that old friends suffer

And that their suffering doesn't get any better, and that it hurts us, hurls

The us that would have been us against the gnomic sarcophagus that passes

For literate speech among the literately speechy (the very very few mind you)

So that testimonies linger on the stand, nowhere to go, no woman no man

Nothing to stand for, them, nothing, nowhere to stand, the words alone

Slipping past slippage into the banded heterodox of meaning as it is meant

As it is meant as it means as it is sometimes meant to happen, a palimpsest

A palimpsest of all that, containing all that, of all that containing all that

But with nothing in it with nothing in it nothing nothing with nothing in it

That's where the age goes, a kind of pen in an inkwell, well, you know

What is meant, the right hand tied to the left hand and neither of them right

Neither of them getting out of bounds (bondage (political bondage (political

Bondage (bondage political to this time (this noontime))))) fleecing time

Of meaning as if either had time to be but no, there're only gerundless fucks

Sqleaking over the of into the prepositionless abetment sequestering quest

Ions that slick up the slide of flate, glaring over the frost flick frame of form

(No form!) as if treatment had a way to go until tomorrow and the eager

Ones the ones not beaten out of eagerness (are there any left) have a slim

Chance of sequestering greetings as against the fluck slam dim crape corpse

Sinking into the some (the ones) the some the sad some (those ones) ones

Who can only get up when it's too late to get up who can only get down

When it's too late to get down (or up (for that matter)) who lose just by being

Into the lingering fluck gutter, old memories of the old memories slept past

And the sling hardenable fasteners that clack back on the recurring monstrances

Sleeping, sleeping, sleeping (there was sleep) where the wary clop, an instance

Of clop, as the cakers snake off with the sped slup slangers (those who can speak)

Into the days' worst enemies (the days) and the nights' worst enemies (the nights)

So that memory eats itself like the soil of the enemy and suffering is only the

Answer to the question about suffering and people keep saying that life isn't fair

But saying so isn't fair either (dammit!) so flut the shuck up (maddit!) or sleep

Or sleep my little ones or sleep, or be sleep or be sleep my little ones or be sleep

In the drilling moist moons of noon, the splitting moist droons of bloon, the slap

Shaping itself already (against that (against (against that))) into a fist into a

Fullblown flist claking sluck manch dread where dread is better then death on the

Quantrails of sleep slick stuff (the old kind (still alive)) but there is eagerness

There is eagerness there is eagerness there is eagerness after all we do try

To rip up they sheets before they decay of their own volition their own volute

Volition we do try, but, there aren't enough sentences to go around we get stuck

We get stuck having to share the same with one and with god wouldn't you know it

Just about everyone, not that there is any such thing as just about everyone, but there

Is there fucking goddamn well is, just about everyone, and with them, with them

The we that is we share what is not we, the end, flaking up against us like the age

Of the prophets (the one without projects) (the one without age) (the one without)

Such that (such that?!?) (as if that were possible!!) there's a meaningless word

To follow this one and by god do we have it for you, now where was it, what did we

Do with it, did we ever have it, what did we mean (by that (or any of it)) (flake)

Ok no no-k, no word, no this one nothing to following and therefore no word lost

(Hallefuckinglujah!!!) as against the cancerous cells of what the language really is

And don't let me remind you of that don't let me even repeat it don't let me even say

It (I didn't mean it) god (hod) I hate the fucking first person how did that slip in here

As if there were a one, and as if that one could speak, hah!, nothing could be further

From the flurth, get that through your flucking fled, I did and by glod did that hurt!

Alright, ok, alright, I've thunk we've gone a little overbored, let's reign this in here

Back to mothership flirth (the quacking (oh the quacking)) because treatises can only

Be signed between two people who don't know what they're doing, people who don't

Know and who can't sign (that keeps it safe) such (suck) that it's all a negative

Don't you see, a negative with you in it, one that I created, so that it would have me

In it, one big negative with no positive in sight, nothing to look back on forward to

Nothing other to be to be there (or here (for this matter)) and only sadness sleeps

Out of our wounds as the day winds down into the slippery flap sails slinging rope

Over the side of the dim hope, the sluck track strack slinkers, the real ones, the yous

And the mes, the nameless (all of us) that gastrously glet misspelt, trimpt, slumpckt

And slaughtered, it's that simple, or haven't you been paying any kind of attlention

here

to this

As err as far as far can see

As err as far as far can see
And all live well in err or tree
That swell nor line the can't to be
As well as might as might as we

Then torn from fruit the lock is rife
And small shrill thing a thing called life
That still can be a man nor wife
But the will is chime as chime is life

And there were days when tents were it
And flew from place to place as tit
For that is this and this is it but smit

For the flank thrust of what wanes snore
Be what is first or aft or aft or fore
As all comes down to day and day to yore

44

STEAMING INTO PLANGENT HARBOR

AFFRONT AND ASLANT THE SAME

AUTOMATICALLY YOUR LIPSTICK
BRINGS ME ROUND AGAIN

SLEPT

AND THE TRANSIENT SLOW ONES
CAPITALIZE
ON WHAT NONE OF US CAN TO NONE OF THEM EXPLAIN

SADNESS
OBEISANCE
TRILOGIES OF STRAIN

AND EVEN THE SLIM CHANCE OF GAIN

THE ERRANT SLIM SLOW CHANCE OF
AGAIN

SUCKLES
STRAPS ITSELF TO A

THERE'S NO OTHER WAY
SOME DAY

THAT THE ROCK SINGLE SOURCES
SLYLY
ESCAPE US
OVER THE TILTING LONG AVENUES OF RAIN
(IN THE RAIN

I'LL LOVE YOU
AGAIN

REMNANTS

                              REMNANTS OF RAIN

                                                              REMAIN

                         SEQUESTERABLE MOMENTS TRACK US UP
           THOUGH THERE ARE REASONABLE REASONS FOR
                                             BEING HERE

                    THEY'RE NOT ENOUGH

               NEITHER YOU NOR I
           KNOW THE SAD SLIM REASON WHY

                                   BUT YOU (NAMED ONE
                                        HAVE WITHIN THE SEA
      SPELLING ITSELF AGAINST THE SHORE OF ALL THE SHORES OF THE
      SHORES

               LONG AS HE WEARS A PLAIN GOLDEN RING

                                             SLIM FOXES
                                      AMONG THE PHLOX
                                   WAITING TO OUTFOX US
                             WITH THE FOXED EDGES OF THEIR GAIN

                                             UNTIL WE
                                        WE TOO (TWO
                         COME AGAINST THE SLINKING SHORES
                             THAT BATTER UP AGAINST THE

      THIS IS FOR YOU
      YOU WITH A NAME (WITH A NAME I CANNOT REPEAT
      (EVEN HERE
      ON THIS EVE OF ALL THAT MIGHT IN RETROSPECT HAVE HAPPENED
      FOR (THIS IS FOR YOU

                    AND FOR YOUR NAME (HERE

                         GARGANTUAN TILES
                         FALL FROM THE SKY
                         NARROWLY MISSING

                         THE SKY

                                        THEN ALL THIS

UNREASONABLE

                                    ADDS TO ALL THAT IS

REASONABLE

                              THE UNREASONABLE
                  AND WE'RE TAKEN TOKENS AGAINST THE SLIM
              SLIME OF RESEARCH (TIME'S RESEARCH

                        TORN CURTAIN

                        TORN CURTAIN

                        BLACK CURTAIN

                        TORN CURTAIN

                                            AND THERE'S A WAY
                            THAT WE HAVE OF GETTING GONE
                          EVEN WITH AND AS EACH OTHER
                    THE SENSIBLE HAPPILY ENSCONCED OTHER
                                        THAT IS EACH
                              EACH TO THE OTHER
                                      (AS NOW

                                        (IN A VOW

              OH THE OLD PEOPLE HAVE THEMSELVES

              THERE ARE REASONS (THERE HAVE TO BE REASONS
              THAT KIND OF JUST SLIM HUNK
              OVER THE

AND THE YOUNG PEOPLE ARE THE OLD PEOPLE
IN THIS AGE AND DAY
(AND DON'T YOU FORGET IT
NOT IN (NOT IN THIS DAY AND AGE

                        SO THAT WE KNOW
                  FROM HOWEVER GREAT A DISTANCE
                  THE STORM WARNING OF A CLOCK
                              OR BELL

                        BRINGING US
                        (US AS HARBINGERS
                        TO A (KNELL

TAKING MUSIC
SUCH THAT THAT IS THE THAT THAT THAT IS BUT
NO MORE THAN THE THAT THAT THAT IS
(AS SOUND TOKENING SOUND

(I REMEMBER RUBEN AND MIRIAM
(LIKE IT WAS YESTERDAY
IT WAS YESTERDAY
AND A MULTITUDE OF SAME BEFORE THAT
(I REMEMBER RUBEN
AND MIRIAM LIKE IT WAS YESTERDAY
AND NEITHER DEAD
AND NEITHER DEAD NOR GONE
(I REMEMBER
(I REMEMBER
RUBEN
AND MIRIAM
LIKE IT WAS
LIKE
LIKE IT WAS
(YESTERDAY

AND THE GLAZED

QUAKING MUSCLES
IN THAT KIND OF EFFORT
TO GET THAT BACK
OVER THE BACK OF THE HURDLING

SO STORMY
SO STORMY A KING
IS A THING

(SO STORMY A THING

MY OLD OVERCOAT
IS ALL THAT WE HAVE
TAKEN AS A BEST OF THINGS
A BEST OF ALL POSSIBLE THINGS
IN A WORLD
(A WORLD WHERE THERE ARE
NO
BEST
OF ALL POSSIBLE THINGS

                                      JUST THE ROMANTIC NOTION
                                          THE ROMANTIC NOTION
                                  THAT A NOTION IS POSSIBLE
                          (THAT A ROMANTIC NOTION IS POSSIBLE
                                         AGAINST UNCTION
                                      AND THE SAMPLING
                                  OF DISTANT PLEASURES
                            (PLEASING ONLY THEMSELVES
                                     WHERE SAINTLINESS
                                             IS DARLING
                             (THE SLIMMEST OF THINGS

              WE SETTLE FOR BEING TIRED

IN THE CADAVEROUS MOMENT

                              UNTIL WE'RE FORCED OUT OF BED

FORMING AGAINST
THE BUTTERFLY WINGS
(NOT THE BUTTERFLY-LIKE WINGS
FORMING AGAINST THE BUTTERFLY WINGS
A NARRATIVE THAT WE CAN FIND ACCEPTABLE
                    AND THAT ENDS WITH US PINNED

                      AGAINST THE HAPPENSTANCE
                             OF HAPPENING
                             INSTEAD

                      OF (DEAD

                      THERE ARE THE WAVINGS OF THE TREES
                                     TO REMIND US
                                       BUT OF WHAT

                      AND THEN THE WAVERINGS OF THE LEAVES
                                     TO REMIND US
                             TO REMIND US TO LEAVE US
                      TO REMIND US THAT THEY LEAVE US
                                     (IN THE LIGHT
              AND IN SHADOW OBEY LAWS OF THEIR OWN MAKING

                                     BIG THINGS
                             THESE REALIZATIONS

FEASTING
THAT WAS SOMETHING WE THOUGHT ABOUT
BUT WE CHANGED THE WORD
TO KEEP IT ABOVE THE WASTE

WHERE THE LITTLE GIRLS
COULD SING IN CONTRALTO
OF THE SOPRANO OFFERINGS OF THE
WORLD

(THE WORD

TARRYING DOWN THE PAGE

WITH WREAKLESS ABANDON
WE'RE BE AS CAN BE

UP THERE
IN THE AIR
WITH (

SOMETIMES
IN THE WARMING AIR OF CERTAIN SEASONS
THE BIG ONES
COME
AND

SOMETIMES STAY

CONTRARY
CONTRARY TO TODAY
(TO
(TO TODAY

I FORGET
AND THAT IS BEST
I
FORGET
AND THAT IS BEST

THE POUNDING OF THE KEYS
AND A WISH TO VISIT THERE

FOR THE CONTRARIES
THAT TWIRL ABOVE THE HEAD
AS MERE WINDS

                                                    SCURRY
                                              (FLEETINGLY
                                                 GLOATING

                              OVER THE EARTH'S HARVESTS
                                    THINNING THESE DAYS
                                                   THINGS

                                                 (AT LAST

                  WE WONDER AT WHAT FLOATS DOWN
                  BURYING THIS HERE ALBUMLESS TOWN
                  UNDER THE SOFTEST OF DEAD DOWN
                  AND MAKING BREATHING A WAY TO DROWN

SLURRY

                                        PUNCTURES

          KIDDIN' DIDN' YA

                          THERE'S NO EQUALITY
                          (NOT EVEN THE IDEA IS EQUAL TO
                          ITSELF (IF IT HAS A SELF

              WE KEEP IT GOING BECAUSE WE'RE PART OF IT AND IT KEEPS US
                                                   GOING
                          AND THE CHOICE IN THAT IS A DEFINITION OF CHOICE
                                                AND THAT
                                               (MY DEAR
                                                 IS THAT

                                                       OR
                                     TO PUT IT ANOTHER SAY
                                                   (SOME
                                               OTHER WAY
                                                      (AS
                                                 SOME SAY

          THINGS GO WRONG BECAUSE THEY CAN

          AND DON'T YOU FLAGELLATE IT

          NOT EVEN IF YOU HAVE THE CHANCE
                              TO BE SAD

                                        IN THIS CARNIVAL

OF MISTAKEN MISTAKENS

GLEAMING

OFF THE COFFEE POTS OF DESIRE

(MORNINGS BEING MORNINGS

(AND YOU BEING THERE

OH LORD PLEASE DON'T LET ME BE

MISUNDERSTOOD

I HAVE YOU

THERE'S A CAR OF A SORT / UP ABOVE THE SKY / AND IT FLIES / AND
THERE IS NO EARTH / NOT ANY MORE / AS WE FLY / HIGHER AND HIGHER /
OVER THE SWEET SWEETENING CHANGES / CHANGELESS / AND / MORE OF
A CHANGELING / THAN ANYTHING

AS PASTURES / SLEEK / UNDER THE WARMING RAIN / AS SHEEP AND
PARTICLES OF OTHER PASTURED THINGS / LIE DOWN TO SLEEP / IN THE
SLEEPY RAIN / AGAIN / BECAUSE MORNING WILL COME / AND WITH IT /
WITH MORNING / THE MORNING SUN

I'M THE ONE THAT IS YOU

FOR THE SAD EYED LADY OF THE LOWLAND
SHE WITH HARVEST ON HER FEET

SHE WITH MIND TO REST
IN THE COMING SLEET

BUT THERE IS NO ONE
NO ONE AROUND
NOT EVEN THE GLAZED ONE
(THE GLAZED ONE THAT PRETENDS TO BE AROUND
(SHE'S MINE

OAKS

ARBORETUMS
WITH FLOWERS
AND FLOW'RING
ARBORS

AND THE WONDERFUL THING THAT IS YOU
GRAPES

TOO

(FOR YOU

AND SO WE GET THE PLACE TO BE
AS A BEQUEST FROM THE SEA
AND THE SKY LIES OVER WE
TWIXT LAND AND LANDED SEA

(THAT'S WE

THE

WE

ENERGY
FOCUSED
AND SPENT
FOCUSED BEFORE SPENT
(MAYBE
AND MAYBE NOT
FOCUSED BEFORE SPENT

WE GIVE
WHAT WE CAN

IN THE NIGHT
IN THE DAY
IN THE NIGHT

LET IT BE SAID
THAT HE DID
WHAT HE COULD

YOU'RE THE APPEARANCE OF ME
AND
I'M THE APPEARANCE OF YOU
AND THAT'S
ALL
RIGHT

BABY

THAT'S
ALL RIGHT

FOR NOW

(CADENCING
THE BEATEN KIND
WISHING IT WERE YOU
BEING HERE
AGAINST THE RAIN

THE RAINBOW AND THE PAIN

AT SOME TIME WE HAVE TO LEAVE OFF SWEARING

TO BE ALIVE

AND ACCEPT THE FACT

THAT BEING ALIVE AIN'T ALL THAT GREAT

AND THAT

IT'S TIME

TO DIE

FOR NOW

FOR FRIENDS

FOR YOU

ANYHOW

NOBODY

ANYWAY
(THAT
BEING THAT WAY
WE CAN GO ON
INTO THE HUNTED HINTERLANDS
IN QUEST
OF WHAT WE EVEN THEN WOULD NOT UNDERSTAND

OR DO ANYTHING ABOUT

ANYWAY

WE WAVER

WE THINK

WE WAVER

AND THE HAPPENSTANCE

                    IS A BLESSING   OF ALL THAT
A KIND OF

SWELLING

                                        THERE IS (AFTER ALL
EAGERNESS
                    A KIND OF NOBLESSE OBLIGE
                                        TOWARD THE
SELF
             ITSELF

                                AS IF
                                        AND THEN THE
ENDING

THERE'S WORRY AFTER ALL

THE FALL

THE FALLEN RAIN

THE SINGLE

THE SINGULAR

NOTION

THE SINGULAR NOTATION

OF THAT (AGAIN

                    NOTHING IS EVER AMISS
                    EXCEPT FOR ALL OF IT

                        ESCAPE
                        ESCAPE
                    FROM ALL OF IT
                WHILE NOTHING IS AMISS

                        DARNING
                      IN THE RAIN
                        DARNING
                        DARNING
                      DOWN AGAIN

                        (FLOWN

SWEET ROCKED SENSIBLE SOUNDS
OF THIS I'M SURE
AGAIN OVER THE HARVESTING OF THOSE SOUNDS
FROM THE FEET
(THE BEET (OF THE FEET
KEEPING ALIVE WHAT ONLY WANTS TO DIE (BECAUSE IT HAS TO
IN THE HUTS
WHERE HUDDLING ENDS THE ENDING OF THE DAY
THE GRAY
THE GRAY ENDING OF THE GRAY GRAY DAY (THIS (THAT DAY

                                        FOR A THOUSAND YEARS

                        MAKE ME LISTEN
                        MAKE ME MOAN
                        MAKE ME LISTEN
                        OR SEND ME HOME

                        MAKE ME MOAN
                        MAKE ME SHOUT
                        MAKE ME MOAN
                        OR SEND ME OUT

                        MAKE ME MOVE
                        MAKE ME SHINE
                        MAKE ME MOVE
                        OR ME NOT MINE

SEQUENCES

                        US THROUGH

                OF

                        AND THE OLD OFTENNESS OF THINGS HAPPENING
AS IF THEY ARE NOT THROUGH
                                (AS IF THEY ARE NOT THROUGH

                                                SIMPLY

                                                TAKEN

                                                GIVEN

                                                SHARED

                                                    STORED
                                               TAKEN OUT
                                                   SHARED

                                                    GIVEN

                                              THE BALANCE
                                               IN THE MIND
                                         THE HEART AND MIND
                          THE BALANCE IN THE HEART AND IN THE MIND

                                                 WE FIND
                                                     YOU
                                                      ME
                                                      ME
                                                     YOU
                                          (AND NO DIVIDE

                    I OFFER THIS TO YOU

                          (OTHERWISE
                            (NO I
                            (NO YOU

                          (THAT'S WHY

                       TAKE IT OUT

                          IT'S OUT

           TAKE IT OUT (BE YOU   (THE LONGING

SETTLED
AGAINST THE BANK
OF THE FLOWING
                                          THE SWEATERED
                                                    HAPPINESS
                      THAT (I HOPE   IS YOU

                                                   OVER AGAINST
THE OTHER WALL OF CHANGE

                                          WHERE WHAT IS EAGER
IS
                                                    CHANGE

AND HANGS

                    FROM THE BALANCE
                                              OVER THE SCALDING FREE
THAT FEEDS

                         THAT FEEDS THE FREE (AND (AND (AND

                                        THE UN(FREE (TOO

                         WHERE WE REST

                         DO WE REST

                    IN NESTED SIMPLICITY

                         WHERE WE REST

                                                        (THE TEST

                 THE TEXT GROWS AS A THING
GROWS
                                   SINGULARLY
               OR PLURAL
                                              BUT ALWAYS
ABUTTING
          WHAT NEEDS GROWTH (WHERE GROWTH IS NEEDED (IS NEED

               AND THAT SPELLS

                                        BECAUSE I'M YOURS
                                        BECAUSE YOU'RE MINE
                                             (BECAUSE
                                             NO YOURS
                                             NO MINE
                                        NEITHER YOU NOR I

                         (AND THAT'S WHAT GETS US BY

                                        EYE TO EYE

SINGING

               BECAUSE IT CAN BE DONE

                                             SINGING

[MAYBE THAT'S ENOUGH]

                                        OH ALRIGHT
IT'S TIME TO REPEAT
IT'S ALL ABOUT
                THE WAY TO HAPPINESS

NO YOUR TIME NO MY TIME
                                (NO TIME

OH ALRIGHT (IT'S TIME

                IT'S SAFE
                (IT'S ONLY SAFE
                IF EVERYTHING
                IS GIVEN AWAY
                (WAY AWAY

                (JUST TO BE SAFE

                                        I WILL SING TO YOU
                                        IN ANY LANGUAGE
                                        I WILL SING TO YOU
                                IN THE LANGUAGE OF THE HEART
                                        (OF ANY HEART

                                        I WILL SING TO YOU
                                                FOR YOU
                                        AGAINST THE STRAIN
                                        OF SINGULAR BEING
                                                (FAVORING
                                THE TWOING OF THE BEING TWO

                                        I WILL SING FOR YOU

                                        THERE ARE RAFTS
                        AND RAFT PROBLEMS
        WITH RAFTS IN THEM   AND PEOPLE PROBLEMS
                WITH BEING RAFTS IN THEM (SURVIVING
        AS BEING PEOPLE BEING IN THEM

                BUT FOR US

        THERE IS EAGERNESS

HABITUDE

NOT HAVING

AGAINST THE DULLNESS OF THE DULLEST AGE

SLAPPING UPWISE THE SLANT FACTS OF THE FACES OF THE AGE
(SLAP

BUT
(BUT
AGAINST THAT
THE EAGERNESS
OF THE PAGE

THE EAGERNESS OF THE PAGE

I REMEMBER
RUBEN AND MIRIAM
LIKE IT WAS YESTERDAY

AND MY MEMORIES
SLAP ME
WHOOPS)
UPSIDE THE HEAD

MY MEMORIES MORE SLAP
THAN SHAPE
ME

AGAINST

SHRINKING FROM NOTHING
AS AGAINST
AS AGAINST ALL THAT

WHEN WILL THE TIME OF YEAR BE FOUND
AS THE TIME OF YEAR
AND THAT LET BE

WHEN WILL WE GROW
WHEN WILL WE KNOW

FOR FABRICATION
SETS

(US

AGAINST ALL THAT
                          BEING AS BEING WHAT WE CAN
        WHEN WE DO THAT   (WE WHO CAN DO THAT
                                  (WHEN WE CAN

                                          I'M HARBORLESS
                                              AND FREE
                                          BUT AM I YOU
                                          OR AM I ME

                                          WONDERFUL

IT'S TIME TO TAKE THE CLOCK
                          AGAINST THE CLOCK
            AND SET BACK
                              THE CALENDAR AGAINST THE
CLOCK
                    SO THAT WE LIVE
                      IN THE RHYTHM
                          AND THE RHYTHM ALONE
                                      OF ALL THAT

        AGAIN

TO STRIKE AGAINST THE HARD WON BLISTERS THAT QUAKE OUR SLAKED
THIRST / IS NOT ENOUGH / WE HAVE TO GET THE BIGGEST THING / THAT
BIGNESS GETS / FOR (FROM / US / AND THAT IS YOU

THERE'S HARDLY A THING TO KNOW / AND NO WAY OF KNOWING IT / AND
NO WAY OF KNOWING THAT / AGAINST THE SKY OF UNBEING / WHICH IS
WHERE WE REALLY ARE / NOTHING / NOTHING TO THAT / UNDRESSED

IS THERE AN OTHER WAY / NO / NO / THERE IS NO OTHER WAY / ONLY THE
QUESTIONING WAY / RUNNING ALL OVER US / LIKE THE BLOSSOMS AT
OUR FEET / SO THAT CADENCES / CADENCES / CADENCES ARE US / ARE US
/ AT LEAST

THERE'S NOTHING THAT WE'D RATHER BE / THOUGH BEING THAT / IS ALL
THAT WE CAN BE / AGAINST THE SKY OF IMPOSSIBLE REASONS FOR BEING
(DYING HERE / OR HERE WHEN HERE IS THERE

AND THERE'S THIS IN IT FOR YOU / TOO / ME / OR AGAINST THAT / YOU
MIGHT GET / WHAT'S IN IT FOR YOU TOO / THE YOU / THAT IS YOU / BEING
YOU / AND GETTING THAT / BE YOU / BEING ME / ME / BEING YOU / AS
LOVE IS ALL THAT THIS IS OF THAT / WHEN THAT IS THAT

                                        IT BEGAN
                                AND IT ENDED
                                THAT WAY

THE UNEXPECTED
BEAMS ALL OVER YOU
                        AND THE BLOSSOMING PAST
        DREAMS US
                                DREAMS US AS THAT PAST
        DREAMING YOU

                DRAWING TO A CLOSE
                IS NOT DRAWING
                IS NOT CLOSURE

                AND IS NOT

                                        BUT FOR ME YOU
                                        FOR YOU ME
                                        (THE DAY

        WE'RE ALL HAVE OF NOTHING
        AT A BAD GUESS
        AND NOTHING IS HALF OF THAT
        AT A (BAD GUESS
                AT BEST

WE FIGURE

                THE TENOR HAND
                        BASICALLY

                                ALTRUISTICALLY
                                        ALTO
                        FOR ALL THAT

AND IT SINGS

                        IT SINGS

                                        IT SINGS

                FOR YOU

FOR ME

FOR ME FOR YOU
FOR YOU FOR ME

WHEN IT SEEMS THAT HAPPINESS IS YOU

It all falls away
in the halting motion
that night brings
over these evenings
of halting things

Slender as that may seem

There are quadrangles
even in thought
in the mind
and that is the way of all things
singing
back over the shoulders of the body
toward the body that might be
listening

But there's always space
for space to have seem
at any age
at any time

And darkness is only a language

Full of feral cats

And the swing
of postulate

toward postulateless things
eagerly
as that may be
to be a thing

We know nothing

It's only quiet
quiet is all it brings
and the sequesterless overlings
that only seem to sing
as that thing
and as this thing

Outside all is quiet
Inside

AND IT WAS
A WINDY DAY
SOMEWHERE
TODAY

THAT WAY
THERE WAS
A WAY
TO BE THERE
    TODAY

AND THE OLD WAY
SO THAT
    SAY
        ANYWAY
THERE WAS A WAY
    TO BE THERE
        TODAY

SILENCELESS
AS AGAINST A WAY
TO BE OTHER
THAN TO BE THAT WAY

CAREENING
    SOLACELESS
THE ONES THAT SOLACE
THE ONES THAT NEED SOLACING
THAT WAY
        ANYWAY
TODAY

EAGERLY
WE ABRIDGE THE NEED

TO STAY
       BUT WE DO STAY
ANYWAY
       TODAY

THAT'S THE WAY

HERE WE ARE

HERE WE STAY

ANYWAY
       TODAY

A BODY LOVES A BODY IN ITS NAME
BUT THAT IS NOT THE SAME

    THERE
THAT THERE BE THERE ALL THE SAME

OVER THE PEOPLE WHO PLAY THE GAME
        OF KEEPING THAT THE SAME
WHEN
     THAT IS NOT THE SAME

EAGERNESS IS JUST A GAME
THE KEEPER OF THE FLAME
        THE KEEPER OF THE FLAME
DYING
    JUST THE SAME
           DYING
     ALL THE SAME

OR THERE'S PLACES TO GO
THAT ARE NOT AT ALL THE SAME
NOT ON THE SAME PLANET
NOT ACCESSIBLE BY CAR OR PLANE
    BUT PLACES TO GO
      ALL THE SAME

WE'RE DROWNING IN SHAME
        BECAUSE WE'RE LOSING THIS GAME
AND SWELLING

THERE ARE PLANGENT THINGS THERE
AND THEN THEY'RE GONE AGAIN
            AGAIN

AGAIN
THOSE THINGS THAT WERE THERE
THAT SEEMED TO BE THERE
ALL THE
    ALL THE SAME

THIS IS AN ABSTRACT GAME
    NEEDFUL OF MIGRANT BIRDS
TO GIVE IT A NAME
    TO LET IT FESTER
SO THAT LIFE CAN BE ITS NAME
    AGAIN
OVER THE PLAINS
    THE HILLS AND THE PLAINS

THERE IS NEITHER REASON NOR RHYME
    IN THIS SEQUENCE
OF THINGS TAKEN OUT OF TIME
AND SPELT HERE
    AS IF THEY HAD
SOME KIND OF PRESENCE
    AS A PERSON MIGHT HAVE
IN A SHED THERE
    BACK THERE
    IN THAT TIME

THERE'S NOTHING LEFT
    LEST THAT SURPRISE YOU
NOTHING TO BEING WITH
NOTHING LASTING
NOTHING BEING THERE
NOTHING GOING ON
NOTHING GOING ON BEING THERE
NOTHING
    LEFT
    LEST THAT SURPRISE YOU

THE QUAKELESS
THE MOMENTLESS
THE SPEECHLESS
THE ARBITRARYLESS
THE AGELESS (NO

THE CANKERS
            FESTERING AS THE FEATS OF TIME
THAT GANG

THERE'S
        THAT
                KIND
                        OF TIME

OUT THERE
                AND IT DOES RHYME

THAT'S HOW IT WAS
THAT'S HOW IT IS
THAT'S HOW IT WILL BE
        AND THAT DEFINES TIME

AND YOU AND ME
WE'RE IN IT
AND NO WAY OUT
                        NO WAY OUT
                NO WAY OUT
                        OF TIME

NO

FOR VALENTINE ACKLAND

SHE'S GOING

POOR DEAR

OVER THERE

There are days with flocks of roses
That careen upon the shore
And ways of getting nowhere
That still require an oar

There are styli that we punctuate
When we punctuate the shore
And the cares of euphemistic grace
That come careening to the fore

There is limber that's forsaken
And the less that wants for more
But the loss is all that's taken

And the thing that's never o'er
Is the that that's never shaken
But is put there far too long before

72

Glassine is a color to the wandering eye
settling as that does of all things over
the endless scraped scapes of lingering time

And an oblique way of saying things without
either a you or an I is emblematic of time
with its ongoing sense of rhyme and rhythm

For errant as the day may seem to be long
there are other reasons for reasoning a tome
swept up under the doors of seasonless homes

So that we're happily unensconced in the tribe
as a blessing blanketing us up over time's
trope and that as a way of being here at all

Scrapes us into time's big yawning trap
or there were no way to be here at all as hope
contains sorrow in its hungering hankering lap

with nothing new to say

and with no words with which to say it

there would seem to be a kind of (silent

agreement (one without (any me in it

    for there is a luxury

    steaming over the horizon in vats

    wondering when we will notice that

    (ill as it is (and with us in it

for there is a flurry of one-sided opinion

(all opinion is one-sided at the very best (worst

and that flurry buries all that might've come after it

as it would a rumor of change or even happenstance

    so to have nothing to say would be better

    than all of that (and to be the no-one to not

say it would be like an egret in a chance morning

bearing possibility through the streets of the world

(a cadence (something smelling of the world

and with the world in it like the sound of all sound

oooooooohhhhhhhhhhhhmmmmmmmmmmmmmmmm

the sound of a mother breathing to her child

as she feeds that child (the sound of that child dying

as that mother is killed out from under its crying

(so that to have nothing to say (is all that we can say

for today (anyway (against the harbingers of fate

that decry our saying anything (especially that way

when they'd rather we just die or otherwise stay

(away (from what carves them into themselves

the last of the last of the last of the last of the last

with us wearing thin (here (in it (meaning to say something

but with nothing to say in it (a sock turned perpetually

inside out (without a foot (a leg (a body (or a head

DIODE

this one
the contrary nonsense
the obituary
the old obituary full of contrary nonsense
the corpse
begin

                                                            with the corpse

and there are arguments for common sense

my obedience is not one of them

then the
as the into the from the ground

make it
make

                                                            sense

as there are organs spouting all over the square
full of pigeons and pigeon guck and early morning coffee drinkers
frigging themselves into affordable forgetfulness

                                        think of it like that
                                        like diddy wa did

the contrary organs

the
ok we need more than that
the little ones in organ like resolve over the pastures quaking
absolved
strenuous
strained
and spaced into the thrill of the thrill

                    got the chill

                                there's treacle covered trees
                                        all hovering
                                        over the park
                        in among the treed larks and lovers
                                    larking their quakes
                                                space
                                                  oh
                                        in among the trees

some   times

                let there be times
                let there be power
                let there be err

            let the err be the power

                    now

        let the err be the power for now

my eyes upon your eyes
my thighs upon your thighs

then
sending

                              as eagerly we wander past the wander lust
                                                        of sturm
                                                           und
                                                          drang
                                                       (old school

when literature still had felt
when literature still had literature in it
the quake

of else

and singular moments

glandular almost

                              floating
                              from

                                                                    up

                    you don't know what you do for the remains of love

                              struggle me
                              struggle me

                         struggle me down
there
thank you
something that smells like ground
(dearth

the spectral champ
of tooth on tooth

over these here harbors
vacant of fish
(vacant of having been fished out
(vacant of vacancy
ie here
here for us
in what's left of the left of what's left of the what's left
(not much

but
(no but

lace

or the betterment of
of the betterment

as if all that's left is anything that's left
but
nothing heralded is forgotten
and nothing here is not here
and nothing here
is here
but

battlements)

the energy of the diurnal quakes into the day and out of the night
as the forest is a lamb in the slaughter of the god
over the forest being slaughtered for the lamb of a leg of an idea
of god

it's that much like a trope

metaphor is a noose

synechdoche is a lynching

and the language is at best the worst we've got

and the language
is at best

          form

               comes first

then the mess of content
(best we've got (get it (tight
and that's alright

             my pitiful arms
           are frail for you tonight
       eg

or   not even that

let's begin again)
there are only contraries
it's a mess
they don't live well together
(supplicants
before a tropal mote)
scapes (as we often say
before an autumnal scape (all that's left (these (other (days

       chill me baby

       chill me baby

       let's go

              that's
              what
              knows
              (nose

threads

the sentience of

what's

always

lost

(otherwise

not

sentience

                                 tombs

                                                       thumbs

wombs

                                                         whom

                                of

me 'n'

the dead ones
quake
shake
they're already (already (already   dead

a loaf

and then the lines were longer
in the quaking of the breath of dead spring being the thing
that was then the glowing of the growing of the being of the thing
that that was the thing and then

ooops

and there was
the special unity of your love and of mine and
the (better leave it that way

the way of the things that mount up in your dancing smile
over top of a body that also smiles (and laughs (and bes
as that were the thing

then
there

          over there there is space for another
          but that other is not another
          not an other
          there is no other
          there is never an other
          never any other

          and don't you fucking forget it)

as much of a strain as that might be for you

        we only remember
        the symbolic utterances
        of our elders
        when they hurt us

        and they always do

        and so we investigate

and let that be that
all over that
clinging

as that
is

that

        there
        's
        nothing

        nuttin

                    and I give it
                      I give it

                    all to you

dear one
dearest one
dear near cadaver
dear bucket of guts in skin
dear kin
dearest
dearest kin

                    there are forces at work in the world
                    thank god they're on the right margin

                                    and they
                                    thanklessly

                                    thank us

                                        for

                                      staying

put

Children of the Working Class

dear John: how I loved you

how I do

don't ever go away

please (dear John (stay

I'm the pathos in my own heart
and that's how it starts
and the starting is in the morning at something-or-other Joy Street
and it never goes away
(not today
it never goes away

the learning
(the pathos in the heart (is here to stay

gosh

don't me
remember my friend

the rhythmical cadence
that does not end

there's nothing that isn't
even what was (is
even what will be (is

we ourselves
are the circumference
of the known world

its spiral

and its girl

as all is understood
nothing is forgiven

nor need be

in the bee garden
begotten
with betoken

tea things

                        for your I love you
                           just like that
                           just like that

                           just like that

                           and lie
                           sweet one

                           just like that

my eye upon your eye
            today
my thigh upon your thigh
            today
               and always

          sweet trenchant one

                      being as you are
                  a woman be a woman
                  and a man be a man

               there's a funky season comin'
                         honey

                         and

           theatre
           thrombosis
           trombones
             tea
      necks over the harbor
      the greasy harbor

goin' up in smoke

there
's time

sometimes people's quakes
and quakes
sometimes
quakes
is bein' people

shakin'

I don't just want to know you
I don't just want to get to know you
I don't just want to get to know you better
I don't just want to get to know you better now

I want to be you

                                                                baby

I am you baby
you me

too

baby

rock that participle
swing that ship

                    sound
                is the harbor
                of the soul

                                    there are places to travel
                                and long places to travel
                            and long long places to get there

                                            and they

  they

                                                        they

                                                  they have
                                                  they have
                                                  us in them

                                                  us in them

                                                            we

                                                    the we
                                                    the we

                              not good enough to be elsewhere

                    unhh)

that
factory

                                                        the up

the sectionable things that are only looking like things
so busy looking like things that they can
't possibly be)

things

not up

not up things

for you

for your for your for you
                              (but
                        who are you)

under the tired
tired

the nouns
pushing the verbs
down

the hate
pushing the love

down

into the coffee grounds

(the ground (ground

                                        albeit

somewhat

happen
stance

the that

ok

the the

(remember that

                    and the meaning in it)
                    the way the words leapt

                                        leapt

                                        leapt

somewhere

there is no where
there is no somewhere
only the other side of the space where there is neither somewhere
nor where

the here

the (very provisional

here

                                                    feeling
                                          is the coefficient of
                                                      change

never forget that

                                    and nothing is forgotten

                    on either side of the page

                            for now

                            for then

                              and

most importantly

                    for the distance between

                                                          no left side

    no right side
                              no brain

only the ever
the ever
again

                              's
                            long

                              's
                            there
                              's

                            you
                            you
                            you
                            you
                            you

                                                          in it

                                                          over

                                                          again

for there is nothing of me but you

and nothing of you but

but I dare not speak for you

(for I am not even I

(again

                                                      there's
                                                      only pain

                                                      again

        sopping up the morrow like it was the stuff of today
                        what d' you say
                          it's your
                            day

                                                                    and again

a stroke

the one of the moment (the one of the stroked moment
with the stroked moment
                              in it
                                          a casualty of the past
                                          as the past always is
                                                    the casualty
                                                              of

                                                      the

                                                      past

remember me as a drain

a drain

that sucked the words

out of the sky

and into

nothing

there being no drain no sky no any no anything

                              but

                    maybe

                    yo

y

yo

you

again
the

stain
the strain
that speaks itself

again

for you

then

there is no other shore
there is no shore
no other shore
no shore to get to from this shore
this no shore
to (no other shore

get there

alone
as a statistic
might be alone

there's only the skirt
of reality
pressing in (down
and (again
and (happily again

                                          where we are
                                              (again
                                          here (again

                                              the we
                                            the ones
                                              the we

                                        that we are
                                            the we

            the people

                                  wishing on a dream

follow on a star
                            be the mountain in my dream

the skull upon a star
                    the star
                    the people
                    the people

            in (as

            a star

                              there were a way to
                                              be
                                      that dream

            the semblance the semblance of that dream
                                            being
                                  wishing on that

far

WE'RE MOVING FORWARD DOWN THE THEN
AS IF THE PULPIT HAD A WHEN
                    (IT DOESN'T

AND THEN

SO SAD)

THE DILIGENT CHILDREN OF THE HUFFING
TAKEN
                            SCARFED
AND THERE IS NO WHEN

SO THE OLD DAYS ARE BEST UNGOTTEN

TAKE THAT OUT AND SHOOT THAT FUCKING WHEN
            HEREABOUTS
                        WHEREABOUTS
        THE THEN
                            (AS IF THERE WERE
A
THEN

SLOUGH ME
    SORT ME
            TAKE ME BACK IN AGAIN

BUT BE IT ME
            BE IT ME BACK IN AGAIN
                                THEN

SOLSTICE

THE STRINGER FOR THE FAMILY FOOL

TAKEN OUT AS FOOL AND SHOT
EARLY ON

(ON

WHERE THERE IS NO EIDERDOWN (NO SPACE
UP KEPT
FOR SELF OR DOWN

AND AGAIN   THEN
AND THEN   AGAIN
THE SPACES
THEY
THAT TELL
THE TRUTH   THE TRUTHS
SUCH AS SUCH CAN BE TOLD IN WORD OR

EVEN

DEED

WHEN

WE SPEAK
WE SPEND

THRALLDOM

CONTRARIES

NO E

NO LGEA

NO LG

NO LEGAL CHANGE

IT

'S

TOO

LATE

TO HIDIN' OUT

96

for Fernanda

for the being there
for the being here
for the being her (as it were (in a theater

it's all solace
it's all solace after all
and being together

beyond the thrall

the end is always the beginning
you know that

or

perhaps you don't know that
but you are

that

there is no beginning after all

no end after all

and no end in a beginning
no beginning in an end

only
these feelings
that beget you

if they do

somehow
there is no other
nor no somehow for that matter

(you know

and me I'm in you but only as a cadenceless bit of thought
as

friendship

as

that

and the dark movement of the waters raining down
the
                                        umbrella
as water
actually
as water itself

over water

                                        from you I seek only guidance

                                                as water seeks
                                                its lowest level

                                        the way to what can be seen

rake me
it's a matter of gardenable trust
as
that

                                        or there are ordurable people
                                               thinking otherwise
                                                       of what
                                                     we might
                                                    otherwise
                                                  have been

had there been an otherwise

between us

                        cadenceless

                             why

upbent
                                               toward the sky
                                              the impending sky

                        why

                                        so as I couldn't take it
                                                         back
                                                    and give
                                                    it back
                                                        to

                                        anyone

                                                                    that's
                                                                     that

         there's there

                                                    we're here

         or and

         parade

         and

         semblance

         and

                                                            then one cares for one
                                                                as a distant star
                                                             cares for a near star
                                                                               as

                                                                    a distant scar

                                                                      cares for

                                                                    a near scar

         upon

         the body

         of the planet

         of the body

of the death of

the body

        of the planet

                                  but

there is you and me
as you and me
and
if
that

is

no

not

enou

e

n

enough
then
where

is

                              enough

to
be

felt

over
the
svelte
waters

of changelings

happily

to have

the we that appears to be us

in

it

curtainable

sweetenable

youable

meable

usable

thatable

thenable

thereable

but

there were quandaries
and we were quandaries
and we were those quandaries
and I love you
sucks
as a coefficient
of what

the what

the

samelessness

I know you won't want this
(perhaps
but giving is not all about receiving

there's only wind

this

is a
storm tossed

sea

(no you
no me)

cadence is a kind of spittle upon the sea
cadence is a kind of spittle put upon the sea

and that
is (me

but for you

no)
me)

I give yourself as you give yourself to me

therein lies the magic of the essence

that that is all
enough
to be

for you
for
or
for you
for
for
for
for

me
(we

104

Thrake ralldom riddle and crash

as rash dillddom is childless and middling and frish

but all is thralldom or crashing and dish

o'er the thingish that takesh all of that thrash

And the then as the now is thin thrillingish death

over the threadest then that wakest over all the that

and there were never any angst or any taketh of trath

but sleepeth is then the slumbereth part of drat

The last is the one that taketh the part hearth

and lendeth all of the health to the maker one over

and all of that is the one that dilth over then with

Such then the with ith taken with the then drover

and all with the overerth hath the then with wealth

being a thing with then then with the then driing flover

106

FOR YOU'N

ING THING WALKER AND DING
AS ALL THAT WERE THEN THEN OVER THING ER
BIUT THAT 'N ALL WERE TAKEN DEN
FEUR TEN THEN THE WE OVER ODEN

BUT EN

AND THE THEN EN

SLING SLUCK OVER SLEND END OVEN SLUCK FEND
AALL 'S IST TEND END ND THE THAN THAT END
SUCH 'N FOR T 'EN SLOUGHING IS THE ENDEN ODER
FRICKIN ZIE ZEN SEND OF THE LADER GLEND (BLEND

AFFER EN TEND THAT THAN T AS IFFFER 'N OX EN
BUTTEN END DER OFFEN COMP ENT SLIFFEN PREN D
AS IFFEREN WAR DEM IMMEN THEN DIGGEN DON

SLOFFEN
SRING EN

AND DEM RINGGEN MAN ALDEN SLOFTEN RING
SLIFFEN DEN STROFFEN NON SLEEPEN NO OHOH DEN
WELL WEEREN WEREN OFTEN THINKING OFFEN OFEN

My thinger are flinglets

I'm admitting this over harlets

and then the trallings of the things that fling

as that is were the then of the e slets

If only there were harlots over then thing

and that that were the more slinger of that then

but 'n all is sloughed 'n that 'n that's taken

down the slide of the side of the then then (you 'n

But slick likes lick to the what of the slake for 'n sale

over the slop harbor that 'n then was the that 's 'n all

such 'n 'n at am is em all of em is ever goin' to em gettem

But slides is the them going own the down slick over live 'em

waken um gettin then that that is all that's getting up 'n

such 'n 'em is gotten to be the then is all them that's in thrall

108

thinken

waldren

spoken'

often

and 'n

if 'n

overn 'n

then 'n

of th' then

as 'n

as 'n were 'n

in 'n

there 'n

was then in 'n

cause at 'n

and then that 'n

then too 'n

was 'n the one 'n

un poco loco

'n than 'n then too 'n

was then the taken there

'n

was 'n the waren't 'n

hallelujah ' n ' n

heartbreak takes the soul

over the slong taker 'n all 'n

was the one taken en in

floff then in th one en in

such in the one taken in all in

'n

sendin all tall is was in en

over the send one over the one in

and that is the end in

as endin is the one that ends in

And is all a thrall a bell
and is all of the a knell
and not enough to tell
that that is all as well

For there is not enough
to stake it to the rough
of be the only tough
summoned taken gruff

But there were oily men
faced with token wens
and slotted up as if amen

Since there is not largesse
taken as the thing blessed
with the wing in the stress

112

OH SINK UPON A TONGUE OF FIRE
IN NATURE'S EARLY MORNING LYRE
SWEPT UP THE FELLING BROOK IN FINE
KEPT MONUMENT OF YOUR AND MINE

BUT WITH ALL SENSE THERE'S DOUBT
IN KIND, AND SENSE IS SENSELESS WHEN
NOT BLIND, THE COURAGE TAKEN OUT
WHEN NEEDED TO BE HEN OR WREN

O SLEEP BACK INTO SLINKY EARTH
AS MORE IS HOPED FOR, NOTHING TAKEN
AND SLEEPLESSNESS COMES BACK AS DEARTH

DEAR ONE COME UP TO TAKE AWAKEN
AND CHEAT TOMORROW OF TOMORROW'S DEATH
AND STAY AND STAY, BUT NOT MISTAKEN

it ends
and then the wind
begins

again

to bend

against the alder tripping
lures of light

114

VELVET

MEMORIES ARE AT A LOSS FOR WORDS
DOWN ALONG THE COAST TOWARD NOWHERE AND BACK
AS A LIST TAKES ITS TOKENS OUT OF THE SACK
AND THERE AIN'T NOTHING LEFT FOR NOTHING

AND THERE ARE TRANSPORTABLE NOTHINGS TO GIVE THEM BACK
THE TAKEN THINGS THAT SPEAK FOR THE MOMENT
AS THERE IS NO MOMENT BUT THE THINGS THEMSELVES
THE THIN THINGS SLOWED AND THEN PULLED OUT OF THE
OVENABLE
TRACES OF SPELT MOMENTLESS GLORY

GLORY BE IT A THINK THING AS THEY THINK OF IT (ONLY THEY
AND THEN THE SLIMMING HARVESTABLE SLATTERED BUNGERS
THAT TAKE MOURNING OUT OF THE CASKING TOWARD THE MISTYPING
OF ALL THAT SLAKES ITS UP AND PAST THE OVERLY THINGING
                                                    PERSON

FOR THERE'S NO SLUP

BUT THEN THE MOMENT IS ALL OVER THE LAST LATENTABLE
MOMENT
WITH MOMENTS LATENT AS ALL LOST THINGS HUNGERING UP
TOWARD THE SEASONABLE PARSEABLE SLANGERINGS OF SUPPED
STUFF
AS EGRETS
                LIKE THAT STUFF
OVER THE SWAMPS WITH THIN THINGS WAKENING UP AND ALL 'N

AS 'N

THEN THE ONES AND THE OVER THE THEN ONES OF THE THEM
TO THE THEY THE ONLY THEY AND THY THEY THYNE NO THEY
CUCKOLDABLE SUCKABLE IN A LIFETIME OF SITUATIONS SLEPTABLE
WITH 'N
THE WEATHER
                AND YOU 'N

THEY
THE THEY

                                        SUPPLANTABLE
AMEMORIES TAKE US ALL TO TASK
                        IN THE MOMENTLESS VERDIGRIS VESTIGES
WHERE

THEN THAT THERE IS NO THEY'RE AND THE STRAIGHT LINE NOW
THAT FINDS A WELL COME DIVISION
                                MISTAKEN AS MAIN STREAM
FOR THE ONES THAT HAVE HARVESTS

OR THERE ARE BACKSTROKES
WITH THE HARBOR AS A PIT PITIABLE WITHIN IT

                                            EATEN
                                                      MAIN
                                STRAINED

AND THE THEN ONES
THE THEY
FLINGABLE THROTTLINGISH EGOLESS EGOLESSABLE GASSED TROTS

            (THAT WAS THEN

AND THERE ARE DAYS FLINGABLE ALL OVER THE HARVESTABLE
MOANS

WITH THEY THEY
IN

IT

ORPHAN
        THE FIRTH
            THE FIR
                        THE FIRL
                THE GIRL

                                BOY ME LEFT OUT

OF IT ENNABLE

SLUNG
SLOT

                    GOT GONE UP THE THRANG TYPE OF TROPEN
DRANG

SLING (ME) A MARROW OF A COW
OR A (THEY) THATTEN FLATTEN THE NOW 'N
BUT 'N

         ORCHESTRAL MOMENTS TAKE THE FLATTENING UP THE
SIDE
OF THE PATTERNING OF THE OFFALING OF THE PEOPLING OF THE
SIDING
WITHERE THE THINGING IS THE THRONGING OF THATTING
      WITH THE GETTERING OF THE THINNING OF THE OPENING
UPPING

FOR TH'OTHER

THAT 'N THAT 'N
AS IT ERE WERE 'N
TOTE 'N
BEE 'N
WE 'N
YOU 'N
         THE ENDEN OF THE THENNEN OF THE THRALLEN
                THINNEN

ENOUGHEN)

THENNEN)

AS STRAPLESS AS THE GOWN

AS THINGLESS AS A NOUN

THE LAST OF THE CHANGELINGS
       THE SHAPE SHIFTERS
   SHARP

SWEATERED WOUNDS SOUND DOWN WHERE
                   CANDY

SAYS

I think it is safe to say

        for A in B

I think it is unsafe to say even to today
that the programmable portion(s of reality of taken
and that the momentary singulars are spoken for
by what is over with (and quite possibly forgotten

as that is the way of the way (with no way in about it
but for the all of us to say that there that is no way
and the endable thing is to be taken with the sway (slay
of the moment (as if it had a moment in it (but

it doesn't there being then the thing with the You or the they
that be as they may personable and speakable to the trumpeting
of so long as it's may (it is (and the slow trumpeting egrets
are a fave to this sodden day as slim slickers slide up the trope

into the mammoth moments of tractable time (that can't be taken
      back
or even remembered for all that lack of matter (as the swelter
      swelters over
and there are tractable then thickets of timeless tomes tracting
      down
from the mere mention of sling or slop or the buckets of them own

to the places (the palaceless places (there are none (and with
      the people
populating the unpopular parts of the town (as the eager ones
      drown (from then
into the slaughtered seeps wither there is when and the thinning
      throps of slown
tling harvest (where there might otherwise have been otherwise
      (or the thrown

trowel taken from the ground and filtered out from the silt slang
        thingings
toward the sept sward then fathomable let's go with the mistakes
        then the wards
of the on inchoate state (the populace is a mistake that has
        grown out of all bounds
toward the caskable desert with sound and froth things winging
        then toward the downs

of flack harbingers with fate flating with the then toward the
        noun of verbless audacity
as if (as if there were were (as if then the slick harbingers of
        flate (slick and taken
over the mounds (slacken (the then (with the thing as the flask
        hidden in the hip sack (sworn
to torn the thing as the when of the that then (but (but it's not
        (and the then we think of You then
the one there (then (with the name (the name as it were of
        another then (and only You You then

to be the queen as that were meant as a meantable thing over the
        sparrowed lawns of these distances
from town to town (bean to apple (as we remember or is it
        rememberable with the thing that is worn sown
into the slocks (only You (of slocked renown (as that were the
        presence of Your skirtable patterns of sloss
with the slingering manys of the slatterning thesisable then of
        our (not parting (as we spoken to the talk
of the town with 'n all 'n (and we don't want to be leavin it
        (not with You in it (the takin down of the down

toward the slorps (for there's all of enough of the sound of the
        saxophone comin down (thankin You 'n all 'n You
it's Lacy tearing up the town (into the small shreds of dawn (as
        I (ok it's I) remember You (ok it's You) as the one

for is there an after of a before is there any any energy of the
        more is there an overt door or a floor
is there an anything or a more (snore (just thinking takes us
        past the gates of only what we can't have (but to the
semblance of the memories of the slings that shake us of quaked
        slaked thirst (word for word (into the momentous
memories of You (there as the one beside (and with listening and
        with listening and with listening and with telling

and with telling to the listening and with telling and with
        listening to the telling and with knowing and with being
        being

such that 'n

ok I'm a admittin I'm a carin for You 'n (all of You (and all of
        You 'n (that bein the memory of You 'n me 'n
the listening and the timing and the taking and the giving and
        the talking and the being talking and the being listening
as being talking and the being talking as being listening and the
        no difference) between the being talking and the being
        listening
for You 'n You 'n You 'n (that being enough and all and that
        being enough and all and that being for You and that being
        still for You
so that this is You (and there is no answerin to the talking and
        the listenin and the (but the bein (but the bein and the
        bein bein
for You (You there in bein town (me here in apple town (with
        apple gown as a form of speech or You up there where the
        waters fling down

this frown
for not being there
not in Your town
not now 'n

and I am in dead (sic (seriousness about this dear tender thighed
        ones (a upon You glaze I plant my thigh (a thing
and then we're swept away into the cadence of the thralling
        orality of the singing singular gaze (we have our ways (for
        there is fortune
as it were wit a thing upon a past if only not thinking of You
        were thin a possible task but no as morning sleeps up and
        asks
us (there is no dawn (apart from dawn (and no dawn apart from You
        (taken as the semblance of all I order from the formless
        past
if I could have but (half of what (I ask (for there are tears and
        tear they do upon the cheeks that have not thought of mine
or pined as that were then the thing that might bring past to
        time (or me to You (if You but ask

and (I (it's I (I wish You only but a mask to take from the me I
        ask (for there are portents all of rose upon the sky at
        last (and lust
a thing we might forget if it should last (alas (and eagerly the
        engines take up the slept halls of freightless tasks that
        bind us
but to what (You well may ask (as I remember You on right hand
        there as spoke we well had asked (and eaten too of repast
        to taken from the slashed cask
and dranken too of from the slim things that surrounded us (and
        You (and You (as asked (the from whereof the thing might
        sing at last
to me (the singable one (he of the petulant pencil (the slodden
        words (the drurds (the hopeful stance albeit askance what
        can't be asked
or lost

like it was yesterday (it was yesterday (there is a river runs
        between us (the Charles into the Hudson the Hudson into the
        Charles
as person into person runs for the momentless pun (the reach (the
        finger on the hand or book that once held book to hand (and
        asks
not that it be forgotten or lost to hand (but put there kept to
        hand and taken when we leave that stand (as auguries are
        all that fill us
of the small (the large (the long (the tall (so as we forget not
        the islands whence our id came to land (and landed from the
        side of this to the side of that sand

oh if only

there are tones that only quake the sand (even where there is no
        sand (and those tones take the land out of the land and the
        equal parts out of the equal parts
so that there's no where where we might might not (might not
        (might not (land

let me remind You that love is a sequesterable thing something
        that is no thing and that sequestered cannot be any thing
        or any lost thing
as You are never (any lost thing (never (will be (any lost thing
        (to eye or mind as memory is the harbinger of fateless
        slang

and all treads water until we come again to hand (Your hand in
        mind

can that be last
(to last

we think upon the banks of rhindable waters wherever they take us
        out of slaughter and into the slept harbors where sleepers
        are all that binds
the slinging of the tropes and the we that are all that mind (all
        that we mind (for there are sleepless harbors too and the
        ones where sleeping sleeps us not (nor binds us
nor builds us to the take of trope and kind (but You and I will
        bind (that is the
time

there's an almost slaughterable distance between what I have in
        mind and what You have in mind
maybe (I'm afraid
but what binds is memory and the moment of memory is bound to
        bind (where what is lost cannot be lost cannot be found nor
        can we find the slot where that was lost (in kind
dear kind

for were there worry nor were loss the thing that pelts the thing
        the think the thinking thing upon some cross that albeits
slates the morn for mornings gloried loss (it's You I'd floss and
        take with me in arm's slim align to trake the thin things
        that fross
into the eagletting air (the one with You there (dear (there
        (such that there is no eagle and not loss and not air and
        not even (You there
but the memory of You (as You there (and that is enough (for now
        (of loss (could it be otherwise
for You are the merry thing that all of me has happened to in a
        toss

                        and take me there (and keep the toss

but slinglets are a harp upon a brow and blown the day with drawn
        hay in slain main things kept up and aloft
so 'n
there's a place for You with me in it and a place for me with You
        in it and a plangent place for You and me in it (if that if
        such if place

should be (but take me now upon Your knee (and hold me there (as
        needs as needs can be (for slaken is the where I must needs
        be
and that is where the You is (me (that is where the You is me
        (please
        remember me

as this You see remember me

Your charming face upon a bench a beach does bend and then with
        all the then the this can end but not (not (then
for slough is take and that is the when of all You've taken of
        what's when (You with the broaden smile upon Your neck and
        then
the thrill of Your speakin to the me 'n (then (as if this will
        not end (this (it will not end (for there is naught
        forsaken
of the token that was willing to be slaken (if only (as the then
        was then the now was now the then was then the maybe was
        maybe the then
just might be then (with You in the maybe of the then that might
        be the then (but could it happen again

slacken

token

but no token will end as token as end as adequate as end there is
        no token nor end no adequate as token nor as end no then no
        token then nor token as adequate as taken (or as token
        (then
it's for You (the singlet (the one You made to harvest all that
        that had taken (and the trousers tousled for the not
        forsaken
but for the this when (with the this when in it (the then
and that was blistering me up the slides of the when to the token
        of the possible (impossible when
as solstice is sister to all You've taken and all You've token
        and all You've been (I've seen

I'm thinking of You
and I'm shaking

my thighs are a form of speech with speech spelt all over them in
        the form of the afternoon and the later evening

when You did not so much speak as listen (and then You were gone
        'n (then
over the nymph like harbors with harbingers of harbors in them in
        the nymphs as the afternoon slunk into the time when
I would not be seeing You again (is that 'n (and the time was
            over to the being taken over by the time that was over from
            the time that never was
or was it over (over from the time that never was (yes (I splurt
            You from that mouth my token for of the things that can't
            be token (taken (or sloughed off before we're saken
as we are without the star
of each other as we are

beautiful talented young one
as You are

I approach You as a star approaches what is far (I approach You
            now as a star approached what is far (and from afar You are
here (this star (upon a grounded star (not from afar (a memory
            diligent as wings that sequester then where scar to scar we
            touch
and are (will there be a time I'm make it on that star (as star
            to star there is a star (or over there there is then taken
            that far star
with willingness (or are

I remember You all of Your like it was it was yesterday Your
            cadences Your physical speech Your being there and as You
            are
the thing that You are (the clothing the bar the people in the
            bar the fellow on the other side of where You are (were
            (and all of what You are
in that You are (and the way You tilted being there as slowly
            conversant things became the things they are
(I remember You as You are

Your touch of madness as a thing that gently starred (Your being
            there (as star (as scar
and the palpable thing of Your speaking as a speaking thing
with speaking in that thing

I'm remembering You as You are

far
too far

far too far

and the single memory of the You is You (taken from the shelf by
        You and viewed (as it were
into the cadenceless (otherwise (slack afternoon
but with You the sociable cadences of being the one taken
        (neither me nor now (the taken one (the thing (the thing
        taken
as if on cue (and held up to view (by me and You (over the
        senseless otherlings as they came now to view (to me if not
        to You (and then
as all at were the clasping of what taken was not taken then from
        view (but
off to the horizonlessness of the harbor where the stickingness
        of the skittishness of the slackness of the viewingless few
could
not
be
You

oh sweet tropism

the tropicality of all emotion

in that only I've not done with You as the You that is not done
        with by You as me as is You (nor You
and the then senseless thinkingness of what is true (for as me as
        You (and then the taking of all of that to the slaughtering
        of the few
who are not me (who are not You (but suffer as the other few

dear harvestable one

I'm thinking of all of You as I sense that this is You and then
        the You that is the all of You that I sense of as You is
        the one You of the many Yous that are You
and then I think of that one (of those ones (too (so that You are
        not forgotten as never being will never be forgotten over
        the harbors of Boston or this here other town
where I hunger and remember and remember to hunger for (only (You
as You

for furtiveness is no escape from slurping happenstance and the
        happenings that happen in this stance (as I dream dream
        dream of You

the other one with harbor writ large as the talent that You are
        and taken from the what is not from others there nor here
        abouts (the ones
that slack as we tell into their trellises to be the ones that
        eons spelt us there for being there

and there alone

126

There we sequester ourselves
along the palm avenues

there we amuse ourselves
as fate would have it in a twist

and the cantankerous makes
of all of us a spelt mask

For you there is only harbor
or the caskless meaning of beat

as we all remember it, up
and down joyless Joy street

But for you there will be morning
as there is evening even for the rest

of the stuff, stolen and all but lost
in the harbor and the rough

So were there other ways
of being than the ways of being other

that would be the way to be, but
there are not, nor could there be

a way of being that, though we think
of all that is not lost as stuff, as

mere stuff, the cradle and the veil
taken for what is not all but lost

but for what is all but taken from us
(the ones who are all but all but loss

Sometimes there are only time of some
that sleight all the hands of taken some

for there is meaning in a drum, a slow
drum beating meaning into dad & mom

There are slack harbors with vestments
that my new friends won't like, not

as this, not as that, and the then was over
from the start of the beach to the start of the when

for there is as as there is there or when
but we wonder of those who've missed it

and those who've taken the token for the nub
Such that there is splice and taken stuff

up the nosed the splice where the being's been
from contemptuous thing flowing to harvest

the harbor that is harborless and unharvestable
as memory is all that it has to ask of itself

Or there is an or of ore that takes itself out of the ground
where speech is ground into dust, and dust into speechlessness

above for the spell of what can't be taken or put down
Or there is the memory of you above ground

the slayed one, with time as token for the broken ground
and the stroked being that takes all but being into frowned sound

The where the we with the we with the where with the we above ground
as sound, for the where is the here that we share in the pound that we sound

for there's only mastery where the thing is above the wound of the humbled ground
slaken, or there were other reasons non reasons for being as me, the one in the
    ground

As we walk into the graves and the hedges there's nothing but the slot wrought thing
    bought
to be the thing that we share as there is an other thing being the there that has we
    were there

only in it, being there as deeply as thee, you and the coral singing of the surplices, spelt
    and grown
from the gown, where the you of the having them both is the token without a booth
    but we still remember you

as hanging indent, the spectreless speechless one of the gowned one taken from the
    froth being the one that slates
and then gets remembered when there with humor as the slaken thing that is
    thingletting from the slow being to the being of slowness

And oh love oh love oh love oh love I need you now, and remember the girl in the spelt
    moment
up against the observatory with the planets splayed like moments for all the world to
    take for granted, as asks

For there is no other being, but the being in love, and the being in love is being over all
    being as taken, as token
that all but the all but was then for all that the being, for the slender or the smaller
    tasks of being were the glowing slowing

the ones with and beyond the garden wall, as that were there the taken thing, the one
    with thing and taken in it, and you and
the not you, as thing and not thing slurping and suffering and beginning and being the
    one of the ending and the beginning

to be slowing, to be needing, to be there and to be therein, as that is the one that is
the one that is the one that needs you now
there being now only for the flowing and the being and the one the one that is being in
the twining of the flowing of the

growing, the spectacle over and in the small magic being of the remembering of the
being of that as the remembering of that being
being you, as all that is you, as all that is happening to you hoping to be you the hoping
that is the happening to be hoping to be you

As there be memory, as if it be as if there were memory, and no being of before nor
after the will
of the being of the memory, of the memory of the will, of the memory, of the will of
the memory, broken into until

there is no slaked thing, no praises, no ring, no that let's me sing, but the slaking
overture, the pound of pounding things, as music is
for there are caskless things, taken for the hill, over the swamping of the car, the
emblem of the all that is the end of the end of the ending thing

Thin, as that, as thin as that a thing, oh sweet cadenceless slaughterless one, on the
hill, if it be your will if it be your will
for there is no other being there here, no wonder that takes the words out of the
mouth of the babes that have not spoken nor spelt

the back taken things that are only spoken, not spilled, as if meaning had a harbor with
meaning in it, a place where one could harvest things
but there is no harvestable thing, no nothing that counts for the with within between
us, for there is us that, that us

Or there were trollops, but not enough, as there are narrower spaces where even
space does not fit, so
there were others suffering a while as the soldier said made the killer smile, with
tweaked ones being for me for you

withal as that being that upon the stand of staunchless particles for the foment of
country and western and song, but

if there's a space with splicing over the harbor then that's the place for you and for
        what was me, before this song

There ain't no nothin' left of the last song, the one with all the You in it, but that's not
        that fault, or the wary way of the stranger
there's being here as that were the one with the overtly being of the strained train of
        thought, that strain of thought, in it

We remember yesterday as if it were yesterday, that's what gives it its name, and
        that's what fall for the sling harvest of naught
tracing hallelujahs for the things that are most up front, take it, be it, in the slant moon
        of harvestable harbingers

that slake, and the that's the that, where there is a that, where there is a the, and that
        ain't being much of anywhere, over much of naught
for there were husbandable tokens aloft in every loft, that night, and nothing slept, but
        all was slaughtered in the blaze of speechless speech, of speech

as such, as cusp, I didn't come to fool ya, a thrall is a being after all, a place to be
        inside the ball of the universe of fate, its casking bait
that takes the moment out of the momentless slinging flask and eats all that's left and
        all that's for nor either after

along the eiderdown slowness of rivers and harbors and being places where we might
        be of a drown, for there is such a happy place
and in it we are drawn to the tokens taken slotted and then there's no terrible sound,
        and no one else had to die, but they lied

Sordid as that all may seem, in the seemly seamlessness of not what would ever stay,
        but there's nothing here that isn't play, the great
surprise, slottering over the world of the with us in it, if that were capable of a being,
        but sense is a senseless thing, always

and wary being is taking warned being over the clasped arms of the seat into the
        bussing to the next town, the next state, the next being drowned
for there are the few who don't even care, steal that, the ones who don't have
        nowhere to go back to the whorled

spaces, and we remember that memory is a think of the past, that being there was
never being there for long, even with you in mind
and that the being there was the slow sloughing of people taken, having a sister, for
ever, or the burnt plans of tracked downs, wounded, handed, gone

For mercy slakes it's hands at the hand of drought, and drought has no hands, nor
mercy a stand, but being there is guilty, grand, too grand
framing the sling harvests that usually take meaning into the stands, where eagerness
is the blotter that sucks up the standing of the grand opening strands

of doubt, or were there had to be doubt, where there is reason as an escarpment over
the placated slings slotted with still hurting, the love you that can't speak
or harvest itself from the words that burnt up to the slot top of marine spaciness
where the words are due

to be paid for, here, now, right now, right here,

oh sweet one

to get back to that, the singular, the shining singular, from place to place, from
thralldom to thralldom, as a way of being grace, as a way of coming back to
you
For that is the way of being in your arms all of the bent night, the swift one, the
tokenable, the taken, and the none of it is true, coming back to you

And mercy is an arguable stance in the face of remonstrance and nonsense, the
burning viola slated to be heard as the one that is not that one that we are of
or, and that is not all, then the one that is witnessed and felt and taken for the body
and the glove, the end of love

I'm a rupture upon a gate, and that gate is you, the you of this very long, the you of
this very long song, the end of, the end of, love
stolen as taken is a word for spoken, that there are words for wary and for weary as
that is the worn moment with the thorn, the thorn that is not spoken

or worn, upon a work, or fabric of what is or might be worn, the torn thorn
So that memory is that thrall, the end of love, the dance, the and the space where we
might have danced that to the end of love, the bar

upon a hill in Tennessee, or there are rapture as the an excuse for being here for being
other than we be, in being here
or to spy upon your as you are the one being you there, over the spliced space where
you have chosen or chosen not to be

from the caverns of the art that will not obey what's left of what we are not, will never
be, and cannot be, cannot obey
over the flasking of the tropes that make us all obey, the you the me the day

For there were heralding and there were heralding as that were the innermost decision
taken from the steps of our irreligion
to the ones that be, the ones that be, the ones that only obey, for that is all that they

are today, slipped up to the taken, the willed, the mistaken, the ones, the being, there,
the ones being the ones being there, as taken, as mistaken
as bait, bent, oblate, slate, straight, as there's a kind of street, and remembering is
remembering it for you (earlier poem

the one, the, the one that's taken over the fall of the moment into the frail thrall of the
stuffed momentless agony, the agon
that has a drink in its hand, and that hand is you, and that drink is, and there is a way
of being that is never lost but is, only being, over there, over all, that

Raise it up, and then it's done, back, back on street, where the you is the one that one
cannot forget, will not forget, there being neither difference there
then nor the slough of the singular moment that has token us for that that street is for,
you, the colden one, but not for not for not for never for long

There is praise as an alter ego to the atlas
at last, the place where the palace meets the street, the where the dog gets harnessed
to the meet, for that is all that's sweet, no

For there is no frost upon the trees, no trees, nor frost nor trees, no forest, nor frost
upon the trees, nor being, nor being left to be
and to be counted with the dead is all that's left, for that's the sending of the spaceless
down below, the believer, in the snow

Do not say there is nothing that cannot be taken for the moment that is taken out of
all that happens an is sworn to be slaked
for we wonder at the moment of your plangent harbor, the smoked time of the slain
meanness of the trained leaving of the one what matters most

As if there were another way to be, there were no other way to be, than this

134

take thrall
umberable

momenters
for or sleight handers

sling
slormerers

gor there are for there
and slat is that then there

as sliff
straken the when of the thin when

with inning in the
slored slinged stringing

for far
far gardens

it's a slow moan

the one that's lost
is always lost
forever lost

    and then again
the invincible defeat

to sling a phrase

from the pardonable
hardenable
    things
that are taken

all thinkgs are taken

as that

for there is wonderment
but always lost
as such

    and the ones lost
in my secret life

furled

                    slowed
from the one that takes
to the one that gets by

and wonderment
            once again
is always a thinkg of the past
like
                    that

tlake it
from the shoulder to the moment
as the moment

            my secret life
the one that cries
over the hardest thingingness
does or dies

slum harbor
                    the slump hard or
            the slaughtered one
the slam
                            in flamed glam

as it were not

for there and then not

as it were an then not an then not

only humor quakes
have it out
you upon the hill

there are momentless moments
full of spit and spit and spittle
and if only you were in it, too

but there's exasperatinglessness

for the one for the other, or for that one
                that got by the other one
in exasperation, for no companion
as a king, with a shovel, and a thing

or there be nothing that is not asking
as and then
                        then the asking
of nothing to be (to be
                nothing (as such

fatherless
slackers
myopic trings
            that slake

importune
impotent thringlets of slot thens
                    where wrens
are all that's cost
slot then
                            wept swept
            up into
the blood upon our hands

swatting at flies
            that fly at swatting
        and that's that
                swat's swat
                    over the

bend of the rally of the
        oh it's lost

so an as I'm a still thinking of an a you
(coupla poems earlier
        being that
              you
over all that I can think of as a
you
        if that be a thinking thinkg
that can be done
        over do you

can't get you

I'm remembering you as overlets

I'm quaking at your voicelets

I'm the loss in your egretting

slaughtering the morselets

that anger the slinglets of forcelets

that trachialets are longlets

from forests, or wronglets that slot

the sling into the wrong you'd

things, or there are orphans in thrall

as that is the wall with whales

wailing over the dead threads of despair

as that were the one that is there

But there were others that can be that

as the thing that is taken for the sling

slot taken from the slotted chair

and there's no where but there's that far

as the one that is there, the one that is not

the one that is absent as a chair, there

slower than a prayer, in being not not not there

For there are graceless harbors, and no one

ever went there, the sling of the slaw long harbor

with the arm and the hand, over taken for the slot

The one with the slaughter in it, alright, slackened

for the moribund speakerless ones of harvest light

slinging for the singing is not taking to be singing

in this land, not while you're still on the stand

Taken to be the token of the one that is taken

to be too grand for the sound that is slow to be man

and the then that was the where were the then sand

It' taken, it's slow, it's a gland, in the harvestable

sense of the land, slinging over slot harvests to the grand

momentless spaces of slanted grand, muffed or lost to the

cheek of the one that is spoken of all but on not spoken to

or there were caskets as ways of getting there, and being vetted

too, coming back to you, silence slinging itself into spaceless spaces

such that that is enough of a spaceless places to be, a blooming, and a
    wanting

sorely wanted, as such, without such, such that without such is the
    want of being without such

over the gardens, where the hollyhocks are just a verb, and the coming
    back to you is a noun, for perseverance, is a place

or there were ordinances of indent, intent, as a fractionless end of
    love, with spacing splitting over the moving of the then there

Or we only know the ends of love, upon a tree, as recalcitrant, as
    being as is the end of love in a gloved moment

that takes that where that might be that, or the other thing, with the
    swarthy being of the beige moments slaughtered

for there are moments, slaughterable, and that is, actually, what
    moments are all about, their own slaughterability, the end of
    the equation

that spits it out, for there is no, there is no, there is no, for there is
    no end of love

142

THINKGS

A STORY IS A MEMORABLE THING
AS LONG AS IT HAS GAS IN IT

LIFE
ALL ALONG THE WATCH TOWER

WITH RINGING THINGS
                    AS PER

FOR THERE ARE FORKS AND SPOON
FORSPOKEN
        AS WILL IS A CLANGING TREE

AND THERE BUT FOR ME
                        SLURRY

FROM TOTEMS
WHERE THE WALL WEARS WELL
            AND LIES TO TELL
FORSWORN
AS WELL

FOR THERE IS EVIDENCE HERE
OF WHAT WAS THERE
                    WITH HER
THE PEAR

STUBBORN STUFF OF STUFFING
BRINGS TO LIFE ITS FIFE
        FOR THAT MOMENT

                        AT LEAST
AT LAST
                AND THEN

BUT THE

FOR IF IT WERE NOT A WINGÈD THING
THEN
WHAT UPON THE BREAST WOULD BRING
THIS SWEAT

        THAT BREATHES
AND ALAS IS ALSO ALL THAT SINGS

KINDLY REMARK THE CARE
THAT GETS A STAR

FOR THINKING OF THE YOU THAT'S THERE
IS THINKING OF THE YOU THAT ARE

AND NOWHERE LESS THAN HERE
                                FAR

SEMBLANCES
ALL WE GET OF
                AND THE FACT

IMMERSED
        THE TORSION
PRESSURED IMPLEMENT OF FACE AND FEELING
THRALLING
                        FOR WHAT WE ARE

THE SEMBLANCE OF A THINKG UPON A STAR

        AND TRACTION
        KEEPS ALL MOTION   IN THRALLDOM
FIEFDOM   AND WHERE WE ARE

THAT MEMORY UPON A BAR
OR
A BAR UPON A HILL IN TENNESSEE

"THEN ALL AT ONCE MY HOT WOE
COOLS LIKE A CINDER DROPPED ON SNOW."

    FOR EAGERNESS
   WAS BORN TO BEND US

CONTRARY TO THE MOTION OF THE NOTION
TO LET IT GO
      FOR FROTHING

WE WRAP OUR LIVES AROUND THE MEMORIES
OF TUNES
   OUR TUNES AROUND THE MEMORIES
OF LIVES

AND LIVE AS SUCH
    WHEN SUCHNESS LETS US LIVE IN TUNE

FOR BENT AS ALL IS ALL WE BENDING ARE
AND SLAKED FOR NOTHING NOTHING TO THAT FAR

We sometimes stumble fool upon the harbor of the heart

enhumbled as a memory is to wane from flux to start

but then as all as nothing is a where a how a why

we sometimes stumble upon the fools we try to live by

But taken as the mortal thing that flees not feels

there are the remnants basking at our trench down heels

in slick array as one is lost to hear from time to tome

and no has answer for the heart with heartless home

For flax is something that we know can almost be

and radiant as a day the night can scale lost skies

art trenches with the sloped traipses getting over ended

As all is trough to slake the thirst that we will see

before there is moment or the sling that up gets high

so taken out it is only each to each at last we' re blended

146

Family day

file sex rage under appetite
and let it no more rule the day
contrary to filthing childhood
miscreant adventures
of father to child mother watching
over us all the caged being
caging as twerps were memorable
constraints from pained doors
and not letting time snicker past
from there to the bottomlessly
constrained pores of shame
burning up the lame home slime
for the token taken blamed
and left lame beside the asphalt
of crinkle shame slime with tomes
as answer for what got us down
on kneed non-fealty but felt
pain groaning groins past the lack

slingering the raining blows
of yesterday's under today's
and more to come the whippings
from the whippings come
and take us all back into non-home
for pain is as slays the dead ones down
to the framed cask dread of morning
with the pitiful fractured possibles
that more will come and come
and come but be not come for now
the slack wrackers of where'd it come
from and knowing not the slain pain
of maybe others' days, nor caring
as pain is pain when all we're wearing
's down

shines

overs

slingets

bodices
 of truth

   codicles
codices
warm from the earth

arth
birth

anglers
   anglings

trothed

slarthed
  morph

or dot egg

take

slake

slacken

brocken

often
en

tawn

150

a token is a thinkg upon a tongue
best felt

                      for being there

as all   as none

     but taken

the throttling
of evaporative senses of time
you want you don't want you want
         you don't want what's

     give
only the argumentative part of the
           being of the
        waywardness of the
bent boys along the shore

                     always
              slander
as a way of getting there

     for

               more
is not taken as more than (that more

for endlessness is a crazy part of speech

that spills itself upon the floor
                    upended
                              even as to think of you

        there
            were
                        to be then

        that

                                                for

but quasi bends the tusk back up into the trunk

all tricked out for the big dame
            following nighttime   (that game

and titular

and angular

and muscular
            as all   in frame
(same

we weep upon the cask upon the floor
                              what's more

            or
can that be the said of the what comes next
                                    or
                                              (or

                it tilts
from time to time there's tilt
                        that takes the heavens
so lingualized
                    out of the gore
                              of the sad before

                    nor
                                        (nor

          that's enough
of the end of all that

the being of the ending of all that being enough
as
the ending of the being of all that
                                        a chore
          (for two
upon the floor
                              please evermore

sling down the then thrall into flate throngs

for listening laces
corsets by the door   (discreetly
                    (for

          vaunted walking / waking / walaking
is that there more
                    a thingk of yore / your

for textualization get is itself up spitting

and the reality is the realization

and there are moments   (frozen
                         (but only moments
                                        (frozen out of time
into
time

as per

the instructions

that came with cerebration
and the flucking congregation
and the stompling asserbation
of the inslipid consternation
that is begetting fibrillation
s)
as the way of slitting
                          conflagration

    is there

such a way as the unmitigated mitigation
slaping off toward the hard fisted fist fuckers
        that run this slump

                                        them'uns

            as it were
there's only

a dream in a dream in a reality dreaming itself
to presentness
                        (but presentable   (no way
nothing here to stay
                the contingent so contingent
    that cause and effect are that dream dreaming
            cause and effect
                                as if (that were
                (could be
                                        (here to stay

cause and effect effectively dreaming the world
        into an acausal effect of past effects

's all comes out of the mind
mind not that'n you don' forgetten

                    and bends it
                               at that

collateral damage
another term for life
and equally
          apposite
    at that

                               fibrillations
                    billings
                                    treacling spoons

    marketing occasion as event

but events are eventless
        and
mind not that'n you don' forgetten
                               that un

if only eros were the thing   (took wing
                    upon a breasting bone's the thingk

and fattens itself upon what flattens then for
sling

as if there were a harvesting
as if there were a cause to sing
as if there were a being
                    being
as if there were such a thing
as if there were ever
                          any such a thing

or if there's pardoning
as each to each it's only that we sing
                               that this thing

                    so for you

(still remembering you
(there
(specifically
(upon that specific chair
                    (april 1 to be fair

                              cadenceless begettings
    're
all that   we might have left of repair
                              the then the there

I sing it
I sing it then
I sing it there

                    (for you
                    (upon that chair

                              but wholesomeness
quakes
and shaking garments the slotted shrill slings
     them thinkgs
formenting
                    at slakes of skates and stakes
                              and things

slom

          for you   (at any rate   (for you
al l
          th e   r   a ge
              of thi

s or a n y   late r   allllll   age

          the page

(this page

                                    scampering away from it
                                                         all
                          toward the dark side of the hall

                                             the heaving

                                         of the being
                                      that being all

                                                    thr
                                                    all

                                                     y'
                                                    all

                                        flimsy repast
                           only taken from your thighs
(sighs
                                             by looking
(being
                                                   there

                           with you upon that chair

and this
            the exemplification
                                      of what
                     but the putrefaction
                        of the purification
        the purification   (of the putrefaction
that is history
bend upon itself

(but it's I
(I
(it's I

(remember you

a more pure thing a poem is than sloshe
sleashing or sleashonging the shrake slose
                        of momentless

                                        (prose

it's getting hot upon a day
and upon a hotter day a day is brown
            and all that's left of or then with
the

                        for grown

when where'n

                        slaken

        tropen
the slinging of the trhallien of the momenen sloun

(my mother's soundljs

                                    (I take you out of bed
                                        (and turn you
                                            (round
                                    (and turn us round
                            (I take us out of bed and turn you round

                                        that's sound

                                        the ground
                        the simplifiable ground of sound

oh sweating mistress of us   (all

                                        trachea

the plethrora
the aurora borealishs

        slinget up upon the groundless fround

and slakes

's 'nuff

                                        but if only
           there's always if and if only and if
                                    and only
                              and if only
                                            if
                              and if only
                                  that too

        upon the unglued past of the pressed waifs cast

my god how they're cast

drinking thoroughly-ish
as if there were that enough-ish
and then-ish
that were the way of being-ish
pulled from the moment of slashingingnessh-ish
            lastingly-ish-sh-h

for glory
is a bent thing
on a stem

                                    be
                              tokened

                                    be
                              taken
                                    be

  kept

                                                        be
                                                slippered
                                                        be

                                                    slept
                                                     and
                                                      as
                                                      be
                                                      be

                                                    reft

                                            of cause and of
                                    and of cause and of cause and of
                            and of cause and of cause and of cause and of
                                                  effect)

                                                    beferd
                                                    bereft

shlo we have a thing upon the shlight
that waters
and sis always nigh
                        to night   (nor to remembrance

            (no (such   (thing

is all over now baby blue
                          unglued
as participle

                        to the pattern   (no pattern
            slept
'n
that's   'n the one 'n then 'n that's over 'n

                    gotten thatten onen
                                              youen

the one that one really wants
seems like easy math
the easiest sort of that sort
                                        really
but
              apparently   (not
question   (mark

              it's 'n be 'n why 'n
one uh don' a know 'n
                          do 'n one 'n
                                                  (no
                                        (no
                                  (no 'n

there used to be ways of being

they might have had like a kind of a you and a me
in 'm

but that 'un
          that's all a gone
                          in in

                  (frown

stapled worn down
stapled down
      qoeted then the one worn down offtlen slong
                          drawan on 'n

the two
              cascading complainers
                  come caterwauling after me
'n why 'n

me noo nee noo more motherin'

(but it's all
(it's all
(it's all
(over now
(baby blue

the one I love the one I feed is you

ome come truee
for that be to be you   (in tis this being

to name you by name
is to name a dream
again
and a dream again
is not a game

and

is

it is not you again

be there
gentle

slarvering

one

that's
tongue

with so
word

  upon

                              the impress
                          of page and pen

                                    (for me
                                     'n me
                                     again

                    but
                    then

there are whisperings in the audience tonight
and they have nothing to do with who is or who is
not
there
but only with the
angularity
of the (many
chair

                    as there were being ways of being
                                  in another country
                                   time upon a ponce

                                          a day

                                         (sweet

                                         (weet

                                         (sweet

                                         (one

                                         (upon a wren

as then

                    that might've been   (send

              dladencelss nightless florthings of

(I wat may nads upon your inner thinkgs
and (oh my
(o (I
don't mind to be admittin why

                                        (slygh

    for 'n

            take 'n

                        waft 'n
as 'n that were 'n bein the one 'n

                                        (then

                    I have my mind upon your thigh
                    and I don't mind admiitten it
                                    and why

                                    'n why
                                        not

                                    'n why
                            notten why

                            (I'm slaken

                            (just try

            now tomorrow looms

    as the quake

                    the slingets

                    the ones with arms

                                        for there 'n

                            take that to be 'n the one that's
gone)

is there a one that's gone in all of this
this singular
non-February
is there a one that's not gone in all of this
February
that is
after all
gone

                                              (no
                                                    (not gone
trumpeting the ones of the ones that's not gone
                  or even over
                              song
          song

                                          just song

(memory makes up for what isn't happening
as it furnaces imagination
and imagination is always (oddly
                  in the past tense

(and tense it is   (was

              suppose

if only there were a one that loved me too
                  let me say that
                                    as a real   (me

                    and be through

but   no

                    there's no-one here for you   (too
shrak
shrake me
s
tloo
upon the szloo

                                                        is'n

                                                        were'n

                                                        be 'n

                                                        that 'n

                                                        blue 'n

                                                        glue 'n

                                                        all

                                                        'n

          that be the that that wrings true
                        tloow

to love is to be dead

              to be dead is to have a chance
                        of flowing

                        blut

                not much 'n

                                                craked
                                              (slinged
                                              (slaughtereded
                                              (tlinged
                                              (the

                                              (ones
                                              (with the
                                              (thelings

                                                in it

                                                  er

                      gone

pestilence is the stake
the gravity of the mistaken braken
                                        wak

                                          waken

if 'n

                    don't gurt me any more
                          done
                            t
                    hurt me an y more
                  don't hurt me an y more
                      don't fuckin
                    hurt me any more

                            I
                          can
                        take it

                      no more

'n

even

that's allen I can taken for now 'n

then the endin

don't be denyin

I'm in love with your
our

with you

slaken

down to your toes

be the be
one

the sling
slake

than
that 'n

I'm in live with you

168

A PALLIATIVE IS A THING
UPON A LINGUAL THING

AND A LINGUAL THING CAN SING
AS SINGS A LINGUAL THING

AT LEAST BEARING SOUND
OVER THE GROUNDED GROUND

WERE THERE WORSHIPLESS A ME
AN IN AND BEING BE, THAT BE

It's 7:44 am in New York City, and there is no city
posed as a nothingness over the harborless entropy
quaking up from, or to, but that's that's 'n too
for the frail quakaing the slim slaughterable making

                              of mating

as if 'n
                that might make the thetic crowns stroll on like this
what am I to do, the other one the other when than that do
over blue harvestable moments tlaken and florsaken as 'n

that one was the other, phatic, crowned and taken as down crown
from the the slim slim slaking for the slim appropriate being down
the then being, the one spelt down, sloughed and troughed as taken
for the momemteles that's the one that's there, as theatre, as clown

of you

                              o f   y   o   u
          u
healing the

happen

stance

there bein no endin of the you en

                              ever   en

don
't touch me

don't come near me
me
don't be me
I'mm em me
amd tat is that that I is me the ais me that I moe over overakkl

don't touh
couthc'touch

                              ever

                                                      ever
                                                      (after all

te

h

the hapy

the happt

the happy oe

the hapy

the happy one

si

si

si
s

is snorkelliong inta you

                                                      dread

                                                      gone

                    for a day

he
the one that is lost for that day iad ais alndls this for the for the
lflingliests for the esllkngsetstn gfof the letingslsetst fotheh ofr there
lar there no one oens eof rthakenee forntnem yhe tyintlgetnrlslsn
oland are of rolhte of ofht e htheakene tgofnroee otelte tientbeing
eofjslth3eand atohte tenadlthene althankenel bakdner of theov fofent
oft t9 be gieng hy elaktnelknteklhoiane 9the taone thakensts
thosthak

      how
      I don't mean maybe
      I don't mean how

        thant's th one t
            t
         with the ehnan
              hand

nobody but me

sequesterqble
gakeable
seu3qsterable
takeable
sequesterble

      my fat e   is in your hands

            (slingable
            myaboele
            mable
            myable
            d9able
            doable
            th

            the

            sheq

the e

te

the sequences
ov the atht alllabamma way
bay

(that

slaughterable trotters

you bitches

and you daughers

of the oh so slaugherable trotters

in the tr
in tne entrancing
t
in the what what me of you

dream
ok)
'n

slate

for I
'm all of you

(all of my life on you depends
(over again
(everything went wrong
(I'm a small
(as you
(and that now that I leave you at at last

(always

for

'm
beindomm of 'm
                    but always

but there's
you
yous
you

you were so marve;;pllous with the
                              you're a

                         pants uupon te floo r

                                        I loved you
                                  but you hatee me
                                    for being you

                    so 'n
                    be it 'n

                  sweet one

                     bro

              from thee each

              from the beach

                     t

              from the beach

is is i

is ok t t0 sa haat

                that

I'm n lor eiyh you

                                             youre the one I care or
                                                    for th oen of
                                    the one I care for you'and the athe oi
                                                        cre fro u
                                                           me

                        that 'na

        slakeddl   e ld ed over 'n at ' n then

from rosy

                                              5h3 slinglets
                                again them rpsu rpsu rpsu
euesjm

            swart

take down the then down town
be the one with the town with the world in the big noun

        or gravitations

                                aq

                                          sweetness
                    over the perfectable ground

as that's mighenen be a nouen

                              fo
                              fw
                              frow

                              nw'
                              wn

                              'na

an

nound

cadence cadence tqkn ov

slotten I'm
I'm

sprru

s
sprru

sorry

taken

you 'n
stitchen

gone

en

overenens

176

being momentless upon a sea

as graspless as the you as me

and then there's me for you the slay

the one that's endless as the glray

andlesless

harnedlelessness of he one tatt that be

;of oridinanccen of thehe the

ange ange angles be

oh quite quiet t

quakes me

be h

be that tha that o

th

the one that bakes me of a

and a

of a

178

femina

contrary

lingering there

slong

pardon

AND THEN WE TURN
WE TURN
WE TURN
WE TURN AWAY FROM DOOM

A DOUBLE ENTENDRE
DOOM'S GLOOM
            DOMINATES
AS DOES A THICK UPON A BROW

EMANATES
THE SLOUGHING ONE OF THE ONE
                THE TWO

FOR WE TURN
WE TURN
WE TURN UPON A BROW

180

REMEMBERING THE THRELL OF THE WONDERFUL MEMORY OF SCAPE

AS 'N THAT WERE THE WAY THAT IT ALL FELT BACK THEN (AGAINST PANCAKES

AND THE SPEND (THE ONE (THE END (AS ALL IS ELASTIC AND FOR (PORTEND

THE SLANK ONES OF THE END OF THE SLILLING FRAIL SLACKLESS ONES OF ENDS

THAT THEN ARE HANDS (HENS (THE SLIVERY OF THE ONES OF THE TRENDS

OF 'N THE ONES THAT THEN ARE THE THOSE ONES THEN (SLACKEN (TAKEN

FUR (BURR (BUT THE ONES OF THE SLOW SLANGERING ONES (TAKEN OVER (EVEN

AS THAT WERE THE ONE THAT MIGHT BE TAKEN FROM THE SLOW OFTER ONE

THAT'S GONE (YOU 'N (THE OTHER 'N (THE DANCE AND HURRY THROUGH

THE DINNER (HURRY THROUGH THE DANCE (AS THAT IS THIS AND THIS IS CANT'S

BE OTHE ONE OF THE OTHER OF THE HOARDING (FLANGED (THE GANCE

AND THERE WERE WENS THAT LOOSENED UP THE THIGHS (MY MY (BABY

AS THAT WERE THE SLINGERING OF THE MAYBE FELT THINGS TAKEN SLOWLY

AFTER AND THEN BROKEN FLOATED FLOSSED AND TAKEN TO ME AS THAT'S

THE ONE (THAT'S (EXPERIENCE (UNNECESSARY (THE ONE THAT CRIES AND

DIES (IS THAT THE WAY IT IS THE ONE OF THE OVER LIFT OF THE LIFE BEFORE

THE ONE THAT TAKES THE ONE ABOUT THE HOUSE TO BE THE ONE THAT'S

THAT ONE (AS HUSBAND AND WIFE (FOR THERE MAY BE NOTHING FOR "ME"

AFTER WHAT "I"'VE JUST SAID, THE ONE WITH THE "ME" "I" IN IT (BUT

THAT'S THE ONE THAT HAS NO NECESSARY IN IT FROM TO BOTTOM PUT (OUT

AND TRAKENED (GRANDED (FRASKED (THAT'S WHAT "I" WAS GETTING AT

OVER THE BATS OF THE RIVER CHARLES (WITH BATSMAN AND BOATSWAIN

GOING AT IT (AT THAT (WOW (THAT (AT THAT (BUT NOT THE THAT I HAVE IN MIND

WITH YOU (HAVE IT YOUR WAY OVER THE MONTH THAT MIGHT BE MAY

FOR A WHILE (GONE (STILED (SOMEWHAT SENILE (OR FOR THE SLINGED STRAY

BEING ALL OF THE BEING OF THE ALL OF THE BEING THAT WAY ('S 'KAY ('NAY

AND THE BULLETS FRISK OVER THE TOPS OF THE HARBORLESS SLOP THRINGINGNESS

THAT TAKES THE FROM TO THE BEING OF THE RINGING OF THE THRILLING THAT IS THAT

(THE (USUAL WAY (AND IT'S ALL THAT WAY ('MEMBER (SO 'SCUSE ME 'N ALL 'N THAT'S THE WAY OF THE HEARTBREAK HERE I COME (FROM (SOME (

182

swarmsy

up along the dew

oh whyohwhyeeh

do that be
        have to be you

sling finnerly
                harbor
        best
                        or dew

as that (ooops
            ass that
        is you

from slingering I have you be
                the magic
        slattern
                                lattern
                over harbors sloshed or warm

as that
                might be

for there is a harbor
        real boats
            boats upon the harbor
                slopping there
                                and
                upon the harbor's
blands   (sands   (glands

                    the one where we shall be

and
                              come
                    along with me

for the slacken is the
                                        slaken

                    too

withal

                              from
the slinger bearver be ones
                              that 'n be there

as ever
                              to more you will cry

don't do don't do don't go way gon't go away
so spliff
                              not lie not like 'n
                    not liken that
'n
                                        no

C – be the one I holden
                    the pme pme one I beholden
          tp

                    to
                         tp
sjale ,p,,u =open to

                              ok
                    of 'n

the sloughering
the me over you
hungering
for you over me

today
this is today's
document

funny
that way

slangeringly yours
    to stay
samelessly
            over

signed

slackened and then bitten by what was token
or taken from the toke of the ticken one (go with it
for there was erring on the side of the sluffen
whether there was sluffen or erren we not knowen

one n onen (that there be heraldable parts of the two n
from then on to the frown that is separating the town
for n alten is a onen (againen (from the train window
to the other train leaving town (in the long long rain

as it weren there were comin down again (in (again
there being chairs for the slingin from the then to the then
slowing down again (and the again (from the slown pain
that's bein drain (as it were again (again (but not again

that's the part that laughters to the faf rafters (with
the mistakes la left in to represent the pain (for there is
is (was (is pain (and that being the grain (gain (of the two
that were longen to be bitten (slain (or (or slain (for

we were thinkin of the passen of the train (that day
down the rails of the railing slain (with the bitten drain
-èd one (with the down casket on the way 'n (bein ta'en
to the slayen of the frain (the slim slacken drain o 'en aen

one (never one (no never n (no never one (not one again
the dreat drearth taen to the groun of the slain footen one
that's theat o (that's that one in the earth groun again
frozen (slowen to the moan of the passing of the gone train

186

That's laying back
against the pounded heart
of the speck of the dirt
of the that part

        but and

again

to the end
        of the bend
able part

where slackers (all end

so being it ends

but the speckles of dust
the thrall of the past
the moments that end as such

that

will end at last

                              as such

            and end

or to be enticed
by the blending
                              the end
ing
                    that bends

down by for
                              the river
the fife
                    and the send

so 'n as

'stends

188

it's all over now

baby blue

ONCE IN A BLUE MOON
TAKEN AS AN ACTUAL FACT
    OVER THE INHOSPITABLE HOUSES
OF A BROOKLYN FLAT

    THERE WAS SKY
        CLOUDED
OUT TONIGHT

AND MAYBE THAT IS ENOUGH OF A FACT
    IT WAS
    IF WE ADDRESS IT LIKE THAT

IT DID
IN FACT

    THE CLARITY OF THE MOMENT
        NON-EMBLEMATIC
A THING OF CASUAL TACT
    UNTRINKETED
        LEFT AT THAT

JUST THE SIMPLE CASUAL OCCASION
BEREFT (HAPPILY
    OF EXPLANATION

APART FROM ITS OWN DURATION
        ON SKY
    AND ON TOP OF THAT

THE CLEAR BRILLIANCE OF ITS OWN DRILLING
(AS

    EXPLANATION

FORCING THE MOMENTS INTO DURATION
                    (BUT NOT FOR LONG
              (AUGHT

A ZERO PENDANT

              THE NOT-KNOWN TRACT
CHILLINGLY
                    MORPHOUS
         AS IF IT HAD BEEN MEANT TO BE THAT

BUT TUGGED
A TUGGED
AND TUGGING THING
              WITH TOMORROW ALREADY IN ITS VEINS
                         AGAIN
         BUT WITHOUT STRAIN

FOR A THING SEEN IS A THING LOST
A THING SEEN (THINK
                 AND LOST

EACH MOMENT IS A DILIGENT DRILL

                              AS SUCH
EAGER UPON ITS OWN HILL

MOMENTARILY CRESTED
MOMENTARILY AT REST

              MOMENTARILY AT REST

AND FOR THE REST
                 WELL
                      NOTHING IS LEFT
NOT MUCH OF ANYTHING ANYWAY
              (THE EXPLANATION MAKES IT GO AWAY

EVERY MOMENT RECALCITRANT
                 BITTER
                      IN FACT
IN SOME WAY

ABOUT ITS BEING THAT FACT

SUCH THAT IT SINGS US
                    IN A HIGH LIGHT TONE
                THE SINGING OF THE MOON UPON A STONE
WHERE
(ALSO
IT IS REFLECTED

            TAKEN DOWN

HARP OBJECT

AS CLEAN AS THE LINES BETWEEN TWO FORCES
AS CLEANSABLE AS SUCH
AND THE MOMENTOUS FORCES FORCE US

LET'S LEAVE IT AT THAT
A SORT OF QUICKENED HAPPENSTANCE
FALLING FLAT ON OUR SLICK FACES

ALWAYS INIMICABLE OF GRINNED SUBSTANCE
SUCH THAT THE MOMENT WEARS
THINLY OVER THE VEIL OF FAILED WATERS

LET'S LEAVE IT AT THAT
AGAIN AS THE SLICKNESS IS ALL THAT MATTERS
AND REMINISCENCES

COME BACK TO SLICK US UP THE SLIDES
WHERE TAKEN IS BEST TAKEN FOR WHAT IT IS
WHAT IT CAN BE BEING TOO MUCH FOR ALL OF THAT

IT GRADES US OF THE SELVES THAT MATTER
THAT HARDEN BEFORE THE SELF THAT SLAUGHTERS
THE OTHER HARDENING SELVES OF WATER

THERE'S MATTER FOR YOU
SHELVED OF THE SELF SLOUGHING WATER
AND SOLDIERING ALONG THE WAY

AS MEMORY OF YOU TAKES ALL MEMORY OUT OF MEMORY
FOR THE MOMENT OF THAT TIME UPON THE BED
BEFORE THE DEW WAS DUE AND FLEW

SO SCARILY A MOMENT IS A THING BUT A THING ITSELF
AS OTHERS WERE AND WILL BE BUT NOT YOU
EQUAL TO THE ALL

TAKEN FOR THE FEW

nothing is as worthless

for D (of all of them (of me

nothing is as worthless
as what's been spent
but not used

, honey

my skin is seeing the stars

it's always the other way
not the way that we remember it at all

there's always skin

we're not listening

and then   and then again

for all that
to be taken in

as common   as common riff-raff

and
to
be
                        to the unqualified end

slaughtering the dynamic
that ought to get things going
            if aught won't   again

this is how we remember the slacker pants
the moon above   a part of all that

last year's memories are all a part of we
last year's love its lovely   lone   constraint

and then
it ends   well   then does it end
            depends

slowly
we
are we

            and that is the memory

the things we cannot do

        the things that have taken over from doing
the undone

it's wrung

even from you
from we

        but why this we with no me

it's just the way it is
    the very thought of you without love

can it
     be

let's take responsibility for the past
for what cannot ever take responsibility for us
       for what's past

     aw
        let's let it pass

see you inflamed a thing upon a thing
            my love

   as if only to get away with you
were something we could do

but

no

there's little that can be do to undo the done

there's little that can be done
        to do
       what cannot be done

it's only energy decay
                a flame   a wasted flame
     in a flat featureless field   some day

but not for we

      was it   were it   will it be
               that way
always

     stay
stay

             conflate yourself with we
some day
upon a lone beach in nothing much of a shack
with driftwood sculpted on the shore
and seaweed for breakfast every day

                         may
contrary
      but energy is energy that way

leave we

not alone
   as we

let that not depend
            for there is energy
in an unlocked key

all in a day

        but momentless
           bottomless
              and without a we
what

that

        then is we
           that
   then
                is that we

from now to

           sloped
spinning round in my brain
              again

you yield to we head
in the thicker part of the thicker tube
    remember

is just searching
for what
is
not
there

          anyway

let what's temperate as temperature rise

let the single thing that thinks be that thing

let the moment rise

let the past also arise
                    as it were
                                as a thing in disguise

let the moment arise

let the future then be the sky
                    in this restless dance

remembering you
all falters
                    away
        again

as it should
as it should
as it should again

                    love you

so supreme

            so sweltered
so small
so smallish

                    the smallishest of the ones
        anywhere
                         in between

you there
gasping
upon the sea
of we past

              but no
                                   is no like that
                    is it
                                        a last
bring you down to the memory
oh A you said
              and it struck we like this gong

the knowledge of what's been
is always the knowledge of what's gone

memory is an impertinence
a fact   an impertinent fact
       that we have to face
until it's gone   it's never gone
                    never one

we find you there
a place swept out of history
                  like a tryst in a
                                    in any song

a bird song

let's say it lasted that long

                    maybe not

courage is the part that time takes in this song

and courage it takes to sing it
                    for very long
          or even for not that long
                                        as time passes by
as time passes   itself by
leaving us   the sad wake
of a nonexistent ship   the gradual wake
of a funereal happenstance
                    (we all have our favorite words
such that that is that
                    but not always that
                                        why

a song
a dead song
a harbor song
a dead song upon the harbor
a dead song upon the harbor but not for long
a dead song upon the harbor but for how long
a dead song
a dead song
a dead song washing the harbor of dead song
a dead song
a mellow
a mellow

a mellow dead song
washing the harbor of the harbor for that long
for how long
a mellow
dead
song

but for how long

for you sweet one

let the wings make the wings fly

let the dead birds lie

let the moment be the moment of the sky

let the wings

let the wings

let the wings

touch the
this
sky

for only you are taken as the one upon the wings of this
song / slackened / taken / put here / but for how / for
this / long / so / not to stay / not / not really to stay /
it's always that way / that way / that way /

we think of you

that way

Cannot upon the bent beam split
and can t'other way as well
that that be all that's spelt
and all that's tokened as "ah well"
but there be dreams upon the sodden
the harvestable sloughed sodden few
that take the moment from the sudden
and give it not anew no not anew

As all is lazy in these isles tonight
taken faster than the fastener can
take fright as fright is all that's left
of us of you and all of us and all that's left
of all that's that tonight
            Ah well
let the sleepy sleep not at all tonight
or ever again for that matter
for what is right is not right no no matter
and that is taken and that is put aright
compared to plunder
                but what is plunder
what is plunder as a token of the taken night

The piggage

Let there be lenience on the lambs
the kindness taken as token from them
the sameness that begets difference

over all of the of that was that difference
and all of that difference that that difference
am
      So closeted a thing

           Shrinkage

The ageing of the momentless of am
that thraking of that to the and of the isle
of what
         am
the distillery
of fact from fiction over all the thrillage
of the what's taken and pillaged as what's
am
          the them
             over the them
being the them that am

      Slewage

And there are momentless thinglets
flying frilly over the toplets of the same
though the same be not am
          not am
the samelets be not am

        Casualties really
the real separated from the arm of the am
and the leg separated from the speculative
moments abysmal slicking up the slides
of the trakened slam
      the one
         the one slam

As there were weing down the well

and be damned
          be damned
                    be damned
from all of that
     the hellage
               the foliage down the well
that traken and slepted and slotted and am
the one that thrills the foremost moments
of the damned
               the ones fleeing
over the land what used to be the land
the traking of the land of that what used to be
the land
               and that be damned
be damned

For there is only spillage
          only damnation
     only the damned
               spilling over the damned

slaking

over the thirstless plains of the then plains
looking for words that slake the damned
things
               the ringlets
          the thinglets
sloughing (a favorite word
over the what of the dent in the wind of the same
of the damned
               going down
          only down
                    down
          only

For thirst hungers after thirst
and the moment hungers after the moment
but nothing has dearth
as such is the moment in the hungering of the moment
                         a monument
          not really
                                        a stammering
the steamrolling of the curtains over the damned
of the audience ones in the taken token theater
of the damned ones
                              there
lost

And silvered as a thing itself is not itself

As a thing is not silvered in to be being itself
                                             ever
as that were all

The wailing
                    without the wailing wall

          the damned
                              the penitent damned

As there were casualties and nothing but casualties
upon the streets of what was once a town
                                        an old town
mown down
                the casualties
          taken for casualties
                         and
                    mown down mown down

That's the way of the egress in this here up and coming
town

down
down town

As if there were another way to be

As if being were a possibility

As if a possibility were another way to be

As if being were a possibility
As if a possibility were being
                              well
                        a possibility

But change is chance
and all that it has to offer as such
and chance is change
                              upon the changeless sea
and chance chances changes
                  for all to see
We do see
        One do see
                    They do see
                              You too you
do see
as fold is folded over fold in the wide sickening sea

And there are thresholds
but they're never met
                    there
there are thresholds but not being met is what puts
them there
                  as thresholded a thing is a thing
upon the sea
                        a
        see

We are the memories that are we
Nothing more nor less
                    that is we
and casking that is the what we are upon this sea
shifting as the thing is upon the shifting we
or there were momentless (another favorite word
thinglets that scrape and mow the mown sea
for the energy that it has but is is
                and for the moment that is
                            and for the moment that is

is

                                    we

no
a dirndl upon a casking sea
        ask

AN AMELIORATIVE SENSE
UPON A FROND OF GLASS

A CASEMENT
WITHOUT A WINDOW MAKING SENSE
OF GLASS

THE PLACE
THAT PLACE MEANT
            (ALAS

ALSO
THE STRONGEST MEAT MEANT THAT

TO DIE IS TO LAUGH
AT THE INCONTESTABLE FACT

GLASS BETWEEN THE CROWD AND THE MOMENT
BETWEEN THE FIRE AND THE GREAT
        THAT INHABIT THAT MOMENT
                (IF THEY DO

THERE BEING NO RHAPSODIC FIRE IN THIS
NO MOMENT BURNT TO THE QUICK
FABRIC OF THE PAST
                (OF ITS OWN PAST

WHAT'S SEEN
IS WHAT'S NOT SEEN
        TAKEN FROM THE FLASK

CONTRARY

ALL IS CONTRARY

WHAT DOES NOT LAST IS THE WILL TO LAST
                    (AT LAST
FOR THERE ARE CONTRARY THINGS
FLOWN FROM EVERY MAST
        FROM EVERY MASSED MAST

BUT THREADING GEARS INTO THE MOMENT
IT IS SEEN THAT NOTHING IS SEEN

THE CLARITY
THE BRILLIANT FLATULENT CLARITY OF THE PAST

WERE THERE ANOTHER WAY
                    (SO BE THAT
FOR THERE IS THE PISTONING OF THE
        OF WHAT IT IS THAT'S
THAT'S
                    GLIDING PAST

THE WAY THINGS ARE IS NOT THE WAY
THINGS WERE
AND THE WAY THINGS WILL BE
IS NOT

THE MOMENT IS A CURTAIN THAT CAN
BE SEEN THROUGH
            TO SEE ITSELF
        AS A MATTER OF FACT
                (NOTHING BEYOND IT
                (NOTHING BEFORE
                (NOTHING
                        IN FACT

THERE'S NOTHING HERE
EXCEPT FOR THE GLARE
OF ITS NOT BEING HERE

TO GIVE PHENOMENOLOGY A NAME

SUCH SUCCOR

SUCH SHAME
SUCH A LAME EXCUSE
FOR A FACT
IS A NAME

EVERYTHING SHAKES ON A TREE
WHEN THE SUN SHINES
VACILLATION
IS THE TRUE EMOTION
(SIPHONED OFF

FOR EVERYTHING BEARS ITSELF LIKE A FACT
UPON
(UP ON
A TREE
THE BETTER TO SEE ITSELF BE
(IT ISN'T

EVERYTHING FALLS APART IN THE RAIN
AGAIN AND AGAIN AND AGAIN
AND PAIN
IS THE FINAL OUTCOME OF GAIN

SOMETHING DOLTISH LUMBERS OVER THE HARBOR
AND THAT SOMETHING
IS DEFINITION
NOT OF HARBOR
BUT OF DEFINITION

IT CAN'T BE SAYED

SUCH SUCCOR
SUCH SHAME
SUCH A LAME EXCUSE
FOR A FACT
IS A NAME

212

FLINGING RESOLVE AWAY INTO THE HEADLANDS OF OBLIVIONLESS NIGHT
AS THAT WERE THE WAY OF WEIGHT (AND OF HAPPENSTANCE
AS WELL AS OF WHAT DOES NOT HAPPEN (AND THE EAGERNESS
FLAKES GRADUALLY TOWARD ALL THAT IS LIGHT (AND LINGERS AS SUCH
FORWARD THROUGH THE DAYS OF SPELT LAUGHTER AND SLICK DRIFT
WORN THROUGH (THROUGH (FROM THE OVER MASTERED THIN HARVESTINGS
THAT SLAKE THE FROST FROM THE ROOF OF THE MOUTH (THE WAN ONE
THAT MARVELS AT THE SLAKE SO THIN THINGS THAT BATTER FORTH FROM
TOWARD THE MATTER OF THE SLATTERN AND THE SLIM BARTERING
OF THE MOMENTLESS SLACK THING WARNERS (THE ONES IN OUT OF TIME
THAT TAKE ALL THAT IS FOR GRANTED FOR GRANTED (AND LEAVE IT LEFT
TO THE SLIME THE SLIM BUCKETS THAT TRACK TRACES OF SLOW MOIST
BACKERS FROM THE WHERE THEY WERE TO THE OTHER SIDE OF THE SLEET
BLEATING DOWN ON THE HEADS OF THE BEATEN ONES (THE ONES
WITHOUT OR SKINS AND THEN LEFT IN THE RAIN AS THE RAIN IS ALL
THAT IS LEFT OF THE MOMENT (THE MOMENT WITH RAIN IN IT (THE RAIN
OFF TO THE SIDE OF WHERE THE RAIN (OF WHERE THE RAIN WAS EXPECTED
TO HAPPEN (AS IF HAPPENING HAD GLUE IN IT (BLUE GLUE IN IT (OR
SOMETHING THAT COULD MAKE (MAKE IT HAPPEN (ADHERE TO THE
OTHERWISE HAPPENSTANCEABLE MOMENTS OF CHANGEABLE BLIGHT
THAT EVERYWHERE CURTAIL THE OTHERWISE LIGHT (THE BASKING FLIM
LIGHT (THE WARNED LOFT LEASED LOST ONES (THE ONES THAT WE KNOW
TO BE SLAKED AND SLACKENED AND DOWN AMONG THE HEART FELT
THRILLED THINGS OF HARDENED SLOWED DREAD (FED BY THE MOMENT
TOWARD THE WHAT DIFFERENCE DOES IT MAKE (WILL NEVER HAPPEN
AS THAT WERE THAT (AND THE SLOWING OF THE TIME TOWARD DIFFERENTIATION
FROM THE ONES THAT WEREN'T BEFORE THAT (BUT THAT HAD THAT IN THEM
IN THEM TOWARD THE SLOWED HARVESTABLE ANGELS GONE TO THE TIME
OF THE TIDES TAKING UP TIME FROM THE DESK OF THE OLDER ONES OF SLIM
MOMENTS (TRACKABLE (SLACKED (TOKENED OUT OF THE MOUTHS OF BABES
TOWARD THE HEARTS OF THE PARENTS GROVELING FROM THE FROST BITTEN
MAGGOTS THAT SLIMMER GET TO BE THE ONES THAT QUAKE (BAKED FROM
THE MOMENTS THAT HAVEN'T GOT MOMENTS IN THEM (NOT REALLY
NOT TO SPEAK OF (NOT A MOMENT OF A SORT THAT YOU COULD SPEAK OF
EASILY OR OTHERWISE (NOT WITH THAT KIND OF WISDOM (NOT SO AS YOU'D NOTICE
FOR THERE WERE BURLY ONES CASKING AT THE CORNERS OF THE MOMENTS OF TIME
AND TAKING THAT INTO THE BACK FROM THE BEGINNINGLESS TRACKLESS MOMENTS
OF BEING (IF BEING (IF BEING WERE A THING THAT BEING COULD INHABIT
COULD TOLERATE (OR BEGIN TO LIKEN (TO BEGIN TO LIKEN TO ANYTHING OTHER THAN
THE MOMENTS TRAKEN DOWN IN THE WHERE THERE OTHERWISE OF THAT THEN
FROM THE ONE TO THE (NO THERE WILL NEVER BE TWO (NOT AGAIN (OR THEN
MAYBE (FROM THE OTHER SIDE OF SPACE TO THIS LINGUAL MOMENT OF PLACE
WITH THE TRACTABLE GLOWING (THE THIN THRILLING OF THE TRACTABLE GLOWING
THAT SLAKES OUR THIRSTING FROM THE MOMENT OF BEING TO THE MOMENT OF GOING
DOWN INTO THE SLAKED SINK (FOR THERE ARE HARVESTABLE MOMENTS (BUT
HARVESTING THEM ONLY SUBTRACTS THOSE MOMENTS FROM THOSE MOMENTS
SO THAT NOTHING IS LEFT (LESS IS LEFT (AND THE FORETHOUGHT IS TOKENED BACK
      INTO
THE BRAIN OF THE AFOREMENTIONED THINKING ONE (THAT ONE BROKEN DOWN

FROM THE BACK OF THE DRAIN TOWARD THE SLIM BREAKING ONE WITH BRAINS

LOST AS SUCH (BEING (THE ONE INTO TWO BEING ONE (AND THE TWO INTO ONE

BEING ONE (TOO (THERE BEING NOTHING (OH (THE SLIM BED OF CHANCE AND DEATH

TOWARD THE BIRTH OF DEATH (WITH BIRTH WREATHED IN ITS HANDS AND MOMENT AND
MOUTH

FOR THERE ARE ONLY TWO WAYS OF BEING (AND THOSE TWO WAYS ARE WON OVER THE
HARVEST

OF WHAT IS ALWAYS LOST (ALWAYS TAKEN (ALWAYS FROZEN TO THE MOMENT OF THE
SLACK HARVEST

TAKEN INTO THE MOUTH OF THE MOUTHED MOMENT MOUTHING MOMENTS OF CHANGE
AND STOCK

BUT THAT DOESN'T MATTER (IT'S REFUSED (THERE'S LITTLE MORE TO SAY (ACROSS THE
SLAYED SLACK

TRIUMVIRATES THAT TRAKE US OUT OF THE SLOCKED THRILL THING (THE ONE THAT WE
CAN ONLY REMEMBER

BECAUSE AFTER A MANNER AFTER A FASHION IT REMEMBER US (AND LEAVES US THERE
BESIDE THE SAWDUST

WHERE THINGS MIGHT HAVE BEEN OTHERWISE (IF THERE HAD BEEN AN OTHERWISE
(BUT NO WAY OLD GUY

THIS IS THE SLICK HARVEST HARVESTABLE BY NO ONE (NOT THIS SOON (LATER THAN
THE THINKING CAN TAKE ACCOUNT OF

FOR FORBEARANCE IS BORING (IS IT NOT (IN (AGAINST (THE TANGLED DOT (THE
IMPOSSIBLE MOMENT OF ANY MOMENT

TAKING US FOR GRANTED (AS THAT WERE THE LONGEST THING THAT COULD HAPPEN
(THEN THERE (AS IF THAT WERE THE ONLY THING

THAT MIGHT OTHERWISE HAVE SAVE US (IF THERE HAD (ONLY (BEEN AN US (BUT NO
(THERE ARE ONLY CONTRARY MEMORIES

RUNNING CONTRARY TO THE FASHION OF THE UNFASHIONABLE MOMENT (THE ONE WITH
MOM IN IT (BUT NOT WITH WHAT WE MEANT

NOT WITH ANYTHING RECALCITRANT OR ARBITRARY OR LOST OR SPOKEN OR BESPOKEN
OR LOST OR TAKEN OR FRESH (FOR FRESH

IS THE MOMENT TAKING ITSELF BACK INTO ITSELF (IS SELF (THE (THE TRACTABLE
MOMENT WITH THE THING IN ITS TEETH

AND THEN THE SWAN DIVE TOWARD SOME OTHER HEAVEN (HELL (PURGATORY FOR THE
ASKING (IT'S JUST A MATTER

OF BELIEVING (AND THEN TAKING (FOR FROTHING IS ALL THAT WE HAVE GOING FOR US
IN THIS SLIM SEASON

OF MOMENTLESS FLOSSED FATHERS TRAKING FRORWARD FROM THE FROTH TO THE
SLOCKED MIM HARBORS

WHERE THE LORRORS (THE LORRY (THE HORROR IS MAKING MASKS AND THE SLOWED
DOWN FRIM DIMMERS

AS THAT WERE THE WAY TO GO TO BE GOTTEN FROM THE OLD ONES TO THE SLAMMED
DOWN ONES

AND TAKE THAT (FOR THAT IS ALL (THAT THERE IS (AND 'LL TAKE YOU FROM THE
MOMENT OF INCEPTION

TO THE ONE OF CONCEPTION (TO THE ONE OF CONTRAVENTION WHERE THE TOSSED
THING IS LOST

AND NOT MUCH MORE GETS (HAS TO BE SAID (FOR THERE IS MURDER AS ALL OVER THE
MURDER

THERE ARE TALES OF THAT (HAPPENING (AND A THING IS ONLY A THING TWICE (OR WAS
IT ONCE

NO ONE REMEMBERS (ANYTHING FOR THAT MATTER (WE ARE WHAT IS REMEMBERED
(AND

NOT VERY WELL AT THAT (JUST AS WELL REALLY (FOR OTHERWISE (WELL LET'S NOT GO
THERE (LOST

AS WE ALREADY ARE (OR IS IT WERE (THERE ARE NO TENSES ONLY THE TENSE (THAT'S
HOW

IT'S ALWAYS SEEMED TO BE (TAKEN OVER ME IN QUAKES OF DARKNESS AS THAT BEING

AND WONDERMENT FLAKES ITSELF AGAINST A TREE (A WONDERFUL TREE REALLY (THE
    BEES
FLASKING TOWARD THE SUN (IF THERE IS SUN (IS THERE SUN (DOESN'T SEEM TO BE
NOT ANY MORE (NOT AS THE SUN FLAKES ITSELF (ITSELF (INTO WHAT THE DAY ENDS AS
AND THAT IS (LOST IT (THE B SIDE OF REALITY IS WHERE WE'RE AT (GOSPEL'S OWN
TRUTH (AND THAT TAKEN FROM THE SLIM MOMENTS TREACLING FROM THE MOAN
FEST OF THE THRILL THING LOST FOR (FORWARD TO THE CHEST CHASED CHEST
LOST ALONG THE FREEWAYS (NOT FREE (NOT THE WAY (BUT WHAT MORE
IS THERE TO NOT SAY (NOTHING MUCH (REALLY (NOT NOW (NOT TODAY

oh speckled one
of legs that rhyme

and the glassed in days
taken
out of time

with clear spoken moments
of clear shuttered grace

for there were ways

and the glance
shatteringly
     the other way
that being your way
        to say

but from the beginning
no beginning

                          only this way

this day

the fractionless moment
glistening
taken up from

and the tractless

the softly curvaceous moment
                        one
the taken from
               the given to
                  one
that one

egress
                   upon a sloped brow
being there
being
                      wondering
     how

as all advances are a step back
from somewhere else
               taken

and then wonderment
is a thing of the
                        of every
        moment

the effete moment
shared upon a deck
                        of shards
as if that were tasking
and asking not enough to ask
        of that

or where there might be
        on any other day

frangible

                a token
                                in a sky

momentary
                        tokened
up from what was otherwise taken
for grated moments

but that's enough
that sky

the lingering
the lived by

and fingers

stone
hit the word hard

against the beach
the broken

slake that

       the token

and memory

as a way against
   that

slacker
or rememberer
of the one token
to be taken
      over
   that
       and

there were werewithals
in that particular afternoon
lost
      as such
if such were possible

and that

                                    or the
orphaned ones
the
                    dead tokened ones
sloughed off

for there were
were not
                            that

the silenceless
the

                    and the quiet
taken

for there were taken tokens
                            froth
from

or

        and the angular

the sloughed ones
at angles
from the other not so sloughed ones

                        the them

the that there being spectacles
of the happening
                        the going on
        then

but not there

                  or were there
then
              there

as angles
as the postulates
as the speculative moments
frothing forth
              over the froth
                    moments
                              forth
as were

and angular
          glandular
the the of the ones of the the
                    that
      as

and taken

                  token

what's the

                  or for difference
as a kind of task that were there
from the start
          the having been there
      from
or be it

                  as were

for taken

                  and the slim taken
from the moment of the taking

                for that to be the moment
                            of the taking
of the lost motif
                                        gone
                    then

            over

as such
                the then
the thrall
of the then being the then in thrall
of that being that then
                    in thrall
        if that
were to be that
                    ever
            again

no 'n

it's done as the semblance
but of what
                        the semblance
of a semblance is

                contrary
                        gone
effaced
        as
            not
        as such

for being is a thing apart
from the thrall of the being that is
                    that thing
but the thing is not being
            is not apart

                and is in no sense a thrall

only
thrall

                as it weren't

                                        enough 'n
as
        from the
to the
then that were the space where we
                    were 'n
over to the one 'n
        to be 'n
that one there that that's one not
                'n
as

such

to take one

to be taken

to be taken as one

to be that one

to be
                no

to

no

to be taken as that one
        but

to
                    be mistaken

for
            ok
that's the one 'n
gone 'n
that's the place of the placard
with the non placard holder
                                'n
as such 'n
                is gone 'n

over 'n to 'n
the one 'n
that is gone 'n
to the one 'n
that is over to 'n
being gone 'n
and 'n
that 'n
is 'n all 'n

            done

    but
for the forbearance
of the dance in the cadence of the
particulars
that glance
        over the waters
slanted toward
            the over water

            not that

and there be 'n

as such 'n

                                but 'n

as 'n
over 'n
done 'n
            and 'n
        that 'n
were 'n

the sloughing of the harbors
over the waters in the harbors
and the slaking of the waters
over the slaking of the waters
                over the harbors
                that be that
                        'n that

slay

be

                ok
from
the slotting from the slim thing threads
for the that
            of the ones that be that
        and that
                being all of that

                            as if that

but no 'n

cadence
tripping
from

slow 'n
                        trake 'n
over 'n
          done 'n
     that 'n
                from 'n
                            all 'n
over 'n
          done 'n

as it were the cadences that pick up on
the sloughing of the harbor against
the pillaging of the slow
          slaughtered
semen
                    moments
that beget
          the slimming that harvests
the slow slaughtering of the slim slits
slated to be the ones tha be the ones that

     dammit
          slate
as it were

                    and
it
          were

that it be that
but only for now
sweet one
               as that

                    and then

to place the words there
where they otherwise would not be

                              but
              are
                    as such
                                        if
          even

for if 'n
after all 'n
              that 'n
          then
                        and then 'n

that one

over there
over being the one over there
that that is the one that is over
                                        there
as
              such

          and
                              then
for that 'n
as if otherwise were a possibility
but otherwise
              is that possibility
       of the nothing
              that that being that

over
                    there

slowly
                                being
as such
              among the others
       that being there

                    are not taken
but tokens
from the slim offerings of the tokens
that get us

                         no
                                where

as it were 'n

              forgive me
        fortify me
                         give me
                   be me
              over
                   over it all

and then
as weakness is the end
for the frothing
              and the ending
and the from of the frothing
                                of the ending
as
              it were 'n

         over
as that were the there 'n
              that 'n

         being
beige
              in the country of the kinship
where there is nothing but harvesting
     no matter the season
                                the being
                   the wearing
              and that than 'n

all that

as it were 'n
                over 'n

            done 'n
                                but 'n
that 'n
that's not so for the one of the
one with the quaking with that one
                    in it
over

                for nothing is foe
but 'n

that 'n

gone 'n

done 'n

for 'm me 'm the one 'm being the one
that quakes for the
                harvest

taken
and that then is the one that is taken
out of all of the past
where there is nothing but nothing
and nothing is not the nothing of the past
but the nothing is gone
        where nothing what gone
from the past to the taken
                token
and felt
        and felt
and gone in the felt stuff of harvests

taken

from you

dear one

taken

taken

from you

MAYBE CADENCES ARE TOKENS FOR SMALL GESTURES
CHRISTINA OR IS THAT A CRACKED MOMENT OBLIVIOUS
TO THE CHEER, AS IF THAT WERE HERE AND NOT TAKEN
FROM THE PAST INTO THE PAST THAT WERE TOKEN

OF ALL OF THE LOVERS THAT WERE TO BE TO BLAME
IF BLAME WERE A THING, BUT NO, THE TASKING IS THE THING
THAT IS TAKEN, FROM THE MOMENT, FROM THE THRALL, AND
THAT IS THE POISON THAT HAS TAKEN THE MOUTH FROM THE TOMB

WHERE THERE IS BOTTOMLESSNESS AS A CURIOUS POSSIBILITY
TAKEN AS THE TOKEN THAT THAT IS, BUT NO, FROM THERE ON TO THE
WHEN OF THE MOMENT, THERE IS ONLY THE CLASP OF THE LOST MOMENT

AND THAT WERE THE ONE FOR YOU, OH CHRISTINA, FROM THE TASKING
TO THE WHERE WITH ALL OF THE THAT THERE, FOR THERE WERE NOTHING OTHER
BUT THE TIME, AND THE TIME IT TOOK, AND THAT WERE ALL, BUT NOT ALL.

232

a firm willow
upon a firm shore

entrenched
what is more

past the asking
but before

for there were then
curtailments

of all that that meant
or

but the same slim cask
contained only itself

as if asking
could bring that to the fore

but no
the sloughing

of the wares of the harbor
foremost

or not at all
but not at all

there being forbearance
there

along the wall
down by the river

the water fall
and that isn't all

as if asking were getting
when asking is all

but getting gets asking
and reproves the asker as well

as it should be
as it may well be

for frothy things happen
against the saddening

the speechless fomenting
of the foaming mouth

of a now dead friend
never to die again

or to be forgotten
never to end

sloping off toward the harbor
the sea

where shapes shift after shapes
and shifting lifts the sea

into the miraculous moment
of anyone wanting to be

what they could not be
as all wanting is that way

for what's lost is never found
never to be lost again

the not lost friend
the ever of that again

and the senseless harbors
asking for remonstrance

of some sort
to get sorted out

sort of
and then lost again at sea

as it always is
as it always will be

remember
for that is all we have

to lose
upon the snot green sea

and the ineluctable modality
of the visible

gets confused with we
with how we see

over against the harbor
over against the sea

for that being that is all that

all of that being that

and there is only loss to counter
loss with

there is only loss to see
whether by land or by

for the frail frothing
continues to cask its being

as to ask is to be
for that moment

or for a day
lost at sea

being that day
lost in that sea

that way of being a day
that way of being we

were we a day
were we ever to be a day

or to be

Alan Davies was spawned on the Canadian prairies / and lived in various spots across that country through high school. Then / college in Massachusetts / a year in Boulder / and final removal to New York City. He is the author of a bunch of books / including Active 24 Hours / Name / Signage / Candor / Rave / Raw War. He writes essays and book reviews as well as philosophy and critical theory and the like.
canadianluddite@yahoo.com

ellipsis
• • •
press

1. Fog & Car by Eugene Lim

2. Waste by Eugene Marten

3. The Mothering Coven by Joanna Ruocco

4. Shadowplay by Norman Lock

5. The Harp & Altar Anthology, edited by Keith Newton & Eugene Lim

6. Changing the Subject by Stephen-Paul Martin

7. The Dreaming Girl by Roberta Allen

8. The President in Her Towers by Tom Whalen

9. ODES & fragments by Alan Davies